The

Sweet Potato Queens'
Wedding Planner

ALSO BY

Jill Conner Browne

The Sweet Potato Queens' Book of Love

God Save the Sweet Potato Queens

The Sweet Potato Queens' Big~Ass Cookbook
(and Financial Planner)

The Sweet Potato Queens' Field Guide to Men:
Every Man I Love Is Either Married, Gay, or Dead

The
Sweet Potato Queens'
Wedding Planner

Jill Conner
Browne

Crown Publishers
NEW YORK

Grateful acknowledgment is made to Mary Jean Irion for permission to use an excerpt from the essay "Let Me Hold You While I May" by Mary Jean Irion, which originally appeared in the *United Church Herald*, 1962. Reprinted by permission of the author.

Published in the United States by Crown Publishers, an imprint of the Crown Publishing Group, a division of Random House, Inc., New York.

CROWN is a trademark and the Crown colophon is a registered trademark of Random House, Inc.

Sweet Potato Queens® is a registered trademark of Jill Conner Browne. The Sweet Potato Queens® characters, names, titles, logos, and all related indicia are trademarks of Jill Conner Browne and/or SPQ, Inc.

ISBN-13: 978-1-4000-4969-1
ISBN-10: 1-4000-4969-5

Printed in the United States of America

Design by Lynne Amft

To the precious memory of my dear friend,

Dennis Kennedy Black—

how sweet it was to love and be loved by you.

CONTENTS

Contents

As Boss Queen of the Worldwide Order of Sweet Potato Queens, I do believe that the first and foremost item in my job description is Telling Y'all What to Do. This would be on account of I know practically everything, and even the stuff I don't know, I have an opinion about that will be of great benefit to you. (Of course, that, too, is just my opinion—but there you have it.)

I hope I'm correct in my assumption that you've already read my previous four books, and that you read them in order, meaning that you've most recently completed *The Sweet Potato Queens' Field Guide to Men: Every Man I Love Is Either Married, Gay, or Dead*. And I hope you're in full compliance with all of my teachings thus far. And yet despite everything I've told you, you may still find yourself teetering on the precipice of marriage. Don't feel bad. Almost everybody has to learn everything the hard way, most especially *me*. We might as well laugh about it. Laughter is the only thing that helps, as far as I can tell.

Preface

I don't care if you're eighty-five and contemplating an official knot-tying with the centenarian across the nursing-home hall or eighteen and looking forward to your freshman year of Pre-Wed—I believe this book is for you. Male or female, gay or straight—if you're considering a life-*altering*, if not always life-*long*, commitment to another person, you need this book. It contains true-life experience from the genuine Sweet Potato Queens and our worldwide Queendom—painful and plenty of it. Unless you just insist on learning absolutely *everything* the hard way, this book will save you a fair amount of suffering and provide you with a goodly number of laughs along the way.

I am a fifty-something-year-old Southern, Caucasian, heterosexual female. None of that is to my credit, nor is it my fault—it just *is*—and so naturally, the voice I speak in is that of a fifty-something-year-old Southern, Caucasian, heterosexual female. *I cain't hep it.* But I believe what I'm saying is pretty much The Truth, no matter your personal demographics—just make the necessary mental adjustments to suit your own particular situation. Please note that the advice I offer here, regarding fashion, mental health, weaponry, food, or anything else, is purely *my opinion*. It's not based on any formal training or education, and no voices from another world have spoken to or through me. All I really want to accomplish in this book—and in life—is to get you to think about your situation and then laugh about it.

The divorce rate in this country is way high and climbing. I think a large part of this problem is that there are far too many weddings. My goal is that, after reading both sections of this book (did you notice that if you turn this book over and read it the other way, it's a Divorce Guide?—two for the price of one and one-stop shopping at that!), you will eliminate unnecessary weddings (and divorces) and enjoy the ones you do have a whole lot more. Pay attention and learn from those who've gone before you—both down the aisle and to divorce court—and spare yourself much heartache and tears, pain, and real money.

Maybe this little book will dissuade you from marrying in haste and thus repenting at leisure. Fact of the matter, I don't right offhand know of a whole passel of folks who've had an abundance of leisure in their married lives. You're more likely to be repenting as you find yourself working like an indentured servant round the clock, and most certainly on weekends and holidays. And perhaps you'll learn the folly of focusing so intently on the *romance* of the Wedding that the *reality* of the Marriage—which will follow as night into the day—just plumb eludes you. And believe you me, marriage has got *nothing* in common with weddings.

This book is a practical—and perhaps even realistic—tool for planning your wedding, from prenup to postmortem. I'm hoping you've followed my advice to Be Particular in your selection process, so we won't dwell much on *that* part. (If you haven't Been Particular enough, you'll be real glad right soon for the other half of this book.) If you have any questions, feel free to e-mail me at hrhjill@sweetpotatoqueens.com and I'll answer 'em for you. You can also visit www.sweetpotatoqueens.com

and get tons of free advice, suggestions, anecdotes, true-life confessions, and recipes on our Message Board of Love, while meeting your new best friends from all over the world.

In fact, rather than spending a whole lot of time, energy, and money planning a *wedding*, you might rather make plans to be in Jackson, Mississippi, the third weekend of March for Mal's St. Paddy's Parade. Join the gen-u-wine Sweet Potato Queens for the Million Queen March. You can get married any old time, even the week *before*, and have your honeymoon with us!

The

Sweet Potato Queens'
Wedding Planner

1

Pre~Wed

One of the Queens, Tammy-Pippa, owns an architectural salvage company, Backroads Architecturals. This delicate flower of womanhood goes out and tears down old houses and buildings with her own hands and hauls off the good parts to sell to home-building folks with good taste. (Her husband, Charles, does help out.) In one of the fine old houses she was deconstructing, TammyPippa discovered a little paperback book that no doubt had been hidden away because of the shocking nature of its contents. Called *The Book of Nature*, this thin tract was written and sold in the early 1920s for a dollar. The cover notes proclaim it to be for "the married and those intending to marry—a complete explanation of all." TammyPippa called me immediately.

I raced over to pick up the book and found *plenty* of explanations I've been wanting for quite some time. I was expecting to sleep much sounder in the future after getting all my troubling questions answered and all. I also expected to acquire the knowledge to settle a number of unduly vexing issues for you, my readers.

I knew in the opening pages of the book that I had come to the right place. The author, *a guy*, stated that some *other* guy had possibly exaggerated when he said that the reproduction of the species is the only duty a woman has to fulfill in human society. Hmmmm? That *other* guy gave me pause, I gotta tell you. I'm thinking, okay, fine, have it your way, buckwheat. We'll reproduce 'em, and then we will be punching out. Everything else— *everything else*—is now your problem. Since you're so fucking smart, here's a bunch of babies for you. We're going out for margaritas and then we'll be napping. We've fulfilled our duty to society. Good luck with them kids!

To smooth things over, the author wrote that he personally thinks that there *are* women who have brains as well as ovaries. He was not making a rash, blanket statement of generalization, of course, but simply conceding that it might've happened sometime, somewhere. There are whole piles of women who never have children, he opined, but care for the children of others and thereby may be performing an even greater service than the actual production of children.

What makes me even crazier than reading this kinda crap from some *guy*—even if it was written eighty years ago—is seeing women still buying into it *today!* Young girls are still going off to college with not a thought in their heads about getting an education that will lead to an actual *job* so they can go out into the world as self-actualized, self-supporting people. There are far too many enrolled in Pre-Wed, only to survey the crop of prospective husbands who might be manipulated, cajoled, or otherwise convinced to support them for the rest of their lives—men who'll simply take up where Daddy left off.

I know a little about this kind of thinking. Remember, my own personal financial plan for the future was that my daddy would live forever. I never considered interviewing other potential candidates for the position, and I certainly never thought about taking care of my ownself. As far as I was concerned, Daddy had a lifetime appointment, and his lifetime would naturally coincide with my own. When all of a sudden *his* life was over, there I was with a whole bunch of my life left and no Daddy to finance or direct it. Huh? Now, there's a quandary for you, right there.

So what did I do? The only thing I thought I *could* do—I looked for another man to take his place! Let me just tell you, if you find yourself in a similar situation now or ever, *this ain't the answer.* In fact, it is the very antithesis of the answer.

Now, don't misunderstand me. There's a cosmic difference between having someone who supports you and fixes things and handles all the pesky details of the financial side of life and *believing* that you *need* someone to support you and fix things and handle all the pesky details. Hunny, I am all for sitting on your ass and being waited on hand and foot—it's great work if you can get it—as long as you know, firsthand, that you could do it for yourownself, should the need or desire ever arise.

Because, lemme tell you something else I learned the very hard way: Every potential husband is a potential ex-husband or even a potential *dead* husband, and you need a plan just in case either scenario develops down the road. And sometimes (make that *usually*), whether he leaves your life upright or feet first, he leaves behind a big ole mess, and who do you think gets to clean it up all by herself? Don't be looking around. It's *you*, sweetie.

Remember how you felt as a teenager, chafing against your parents but having to do what they said because of the "my house, my rules" deal? And how as a young adult, you still had to please them some to hang on to their support because you just couldn't make it on your own yet? Remember how that felt? Well, imagine that you're forty and have no education. You quit school to get married, and you haven't had a paying job in twenty years. You've got one or two children and a fair amount of debt, and your husband is a screaming asshole. Yet the thought of leaving is more terrifying than the thought of staying—because you're totally dependent on him.

If you're gonna go to college for Pre-Wed, I insist that you also take a full course in Pre-Death/Pre-Divorce and get yourself an education that will prepare you for the "unthinkable situation"—taking care of yourself and possibly a bunch of children by yourself for a large part of your life. You'll sleep a whole lot better, I promise. Parents will sleep better, too, if they help their children learn this.

Groom Selection Process

Once you're living in the world of reality, you're ready to think about the Groom Selection Process. Our precious Queen Loni had a fascinating screening process, which she used with felicitous results for quite some time. Loni had the great good fortune to live near a very gifted psychic named Bonnie, who could "read" photographs of people and was never known to err. Bob was the guy du jour in Loni's life, and she wanted Bonnie's stamp of approval on him—or *not*, as it were. So the next time Bob came over, Loni told him her daughter, Jackie, had just gotten a new camera and would Bob mind too much, you know, humoring the ten-year-old and posing for a picture? He was only too happy to oblige; it was, after all, a photo of *him*.

Loni then took several pictures over to Bonnie for a "reading," slipping Bob's into the mix. Bonnie spread them all out on a table and gazed at them thoughtfully and mystically for a brief moment, and then, with no hesitation, she snatched up the photo of Bob and in tones dripping vitriol, said, "Who's this prick?" Loni said hesitantly that, well, it was Bob, who was kinda her new boyfriend. Bonnie put the ole *ix-nay* to him quick, declaring Bob unfit for human consumption—a foul-tempered, lyin'-ass drunk. (Don't you love her quaint economy of words, cutting right to the heart of the matter?)

Then Bonnie conjured up another revelation from the images, which Loni had selected randomly, somewhat as a test for the psychic. Bob was the only one Loni had wanted the scoop on, and he had been promptly culled, but in the mix was a photo of a friend of Loni's, a young man, a *very* young man, a man twenty years younger than Loni to be exact. When Bonnie came upon this photo, she picked it up and said, "Your ship has finally come in." She pronounced to thirty-nine-year-old Loni that nineteen-year-old Jim was her perfect match. Loni laughed nervously and left. She had a *lot* to think about now, for sure. She hadn't expected anything like what Bonnie had just laid on her—not about Bob and certainly not about Jim.

In a very short time, Bob revealed himself to be the very same foul-tempered, lyin'-ass drunk Bonnie had described, and Loni ran him right on out the door. And, by and by, young Jim commenced to coming around pretty regular, and he finally convinced Loni that she needed to pay attention. And, well—you guessed it—Loni and Jim have been very happy together ever since. Who'da thunk it? Well, Bonnie, for one.

It's a crying shame that the very gifted Bonnie has since departed this life. She was a wonderful human being and she's greatly missed by all her family and friends, I'm sure. But hey! She would have been a service to womankind had she lived long enough to provide this excellent screening service to us *all*. She could have had a website, and all we'd have to do was e-mail her a guy's picture for new divinations, saving us untold hours of heartache and tears, not to mention pain, money, and wear and tear on our friends. I'd a whole lot rather pay an anonymous psychic a buttload of money to tell me some guy's a lyin', cheatin' sackashit than listen to it for *free* from my girlfriends— or worse, open my own personal eyeballs to what's smack in front of 'em. But no, Bonnie's dead and gone, and we are just all on our own, winging it here. It behooves us one and all to Be Particular.

That sweet Seattle Queen Natalie wrote me with a question about a vitally important issue. She's only about thirty and therefore *larva*, as we know (women under forty are larvae in SPQueendom), but she was doing the right thing and seeking counsel from me and dipping into the vast storehouse of knowledge and experience held in trust by my Queendom. Natalie had had, it seems, the great good fortune of a Southern birth and childhood in North Carolina, but along about her mid-twenties, her parents divorced and her mama decided she needed to move to the other side of the country for a breather. Our Natalie decided that sounded good to her, too, so she loaded up and moved off to Seattle with Mama. For a few years she was liking it out there just fine. She and Mama both have good jobs and share a home they love, *but* . . . (You knew there would be a *but* in there, didn't you? Me, too.)

Everything is fine, Queen Natalie said, but she is 100 percent *not* attracted to the men out there. It took her a little while to figure out why the local guys were off-putting in such a big way, but it finally dawned on her: They don't *smell* right to her. She had grown up around—and learned to love—men who smelled like pit barbecue and the occasional oil change. The men out *there* smell like decidedly unmanly things like cologne and mocha lattes. I see her problem. I feel her pain.

Natalie was shocked to learn her olfactory sense played such a big part in her love life. I was not at all surprised. I've known firsthand for years that most of us humans really and truly cannot get past the end of our own noses. Smell matters. A lot, they say. ("They" are famous scientists in France, I suppose. I worked with a guy once who was always claiming to have read about major breakthroughs in whatever bullshit he was peddling that day. When questioned, he always attributed the breakthroughs to "famous scientists in France.") Anyway, they say that blindfolded mothers can identify their own newborn babies by smell. I haven't tried to do that, but I do know that the smell of a baby's head—and yes, in particular, my *own* baby's head—is just about the most highly addictive, thrilling, and yet soporific fragrance I have ever personally encountered.

When my own precious daughter, Bailey, was a wee babe, I would lie down with her for a nap and curl her tiny body into the curve of my own and fall asleep breathing her scent. I'd drink in the smell of her the way a recovering drunk sucks on a cigarette. If I could've stuffed her entire *body* up my nose, I would have. I can still close my eyes and remember the feeling I'd get from that fragrance—but maddeningly, I can't conjure up the actual smell. (Now, *there's* a great thing for somebody to figure out how to bottle. Forget "new car." If you could offer a mother a tub of something that smelled exactly like her own baby's head, well, there's a fortune waiting to be made right there, is all I'm saying.)

The smell of a man has always been of paramount importance to me, too. Natalie was blindsided by her nose—but not me. I've always trusted mine. There've been men I liked just fine at first meeting, but upon the first close contact—HUP! YOU'RE OUTTA HERE! Not that they smelled bad—who would even go out with a stinky guy? No, they just didn't smell "right" to me. The right triggers just weren't firing, and that was that. And we're not talking about cologne here—we're talking about skin. The particular hot spot for me is the skin in the area where their jaw meets their neck, and drifting on down to where their neck joins their shoulders. I'll hug a guy and give him a good neck snort and see what registers. The right smell will give me a definite "twitch."

Your nose—or at least *my* nose—will sometimes know when a relationship has ended before your brain does. I remember one relationship in particular that was going from bad to worse, but I was still hanging on in that inexplicable way we too frequently do. After an exceptionally bad boyfriend day, he hauled off and *hugged* me, and I stuck my nose in that neck spot and sniffed, and boy hidee, I'll tell you, I *just knew*. We had hugged—and everything else—our last time. He no longer smelled right to me. He *weren't* mine—and more important, I *weren't* his no mo'.

But back to Queen Natalie's question for me. What she wanted to know was did I think that she should suck it up and stick it out in Seattle and hope to (a) happen on the only barbecue chef in the Great Northwest, (b) change her taste in smells, or (c) just become a none (like a nun, only without the religious theme)? Or should she (d) go into debt to finance a move back to the South to sniff out her Mr. Right? I think you *know* what I advised.

So, what we're saying here is this: However many ways you need to Be Particular in this whole Groom Selection Process, you make sure you don't skip any of them. You pay close attention, hunny chile, because if there's anything you don't like about him *now*, I can assure you you're gonna *not* like it a whole lot more postnup than you ever *thought* about doing prenup.

Snag~a~Bride

Okay, I've said much here pertaining to brides, but let's take a little testosterone break and talk about what it's like to be a Groom—or a Wannabe Groom. Where to find a bride and how to go about the wooing and winning process? I imagine this seems a daunting process to all of them—which is as it should be—lest we appear "easy." Rest assured, if we appear "easy," it is only an appearance. We may be readily available and at least initially inexpensive, but there ain't nothin' ever been *easy* about any of us, ever.

Anyway, I think we're all pretty well versed in the cat-and-mouse, dog-and-pony, bird-and-bee world of matrimony in this part of the world. But how do some of those other folks do it?

My good friend the excellent writer Edward Cohen sent me an illuminating article from the good ole *Noo York Times*. Craig Smith wrote the article, but he didn't have the courtesy and forethought to send it to me personally, so Edward gets all the credit for alerting me to this quaint custom of courtship. The article focuses on one of those countries that used to be part of the Soviet Union; now they're on their own but not really much better off, still lacking such basic necessities of life that we in America take for granted, such as running water, dentists, and *vowels*. I swear, the whole name of the country contains *not one single vowel*. This would make for some big cash awards if they happened to have *Wheel of Fortune* over there.

What guys do over yonder is they *select* their desired "brides." Sometimes the man may have actually met her face-to-face and even shared coffee or sheep's eyes or something, but very often, he just spies her waiting for a bus or passing by when he's suddenly convinced beyond any shadow of a doubt that "There she is—the woman of my dreams." Then, enlisting the help of his friends and even his parents, he simply snags her. Sometimes the intended puts up a reeeeally good fight and the elopement committee is forced to concede defeat, at which point the guy simply settles for the next unmarried woman over the age of sixteen who passes by, and snags her instead—possibly as a face-saving maneuver or perhaps just to avoid it being an altogether wasted trip. (This bride-snagging ritual is called *ala kachoo*—sounds a lot like "I'm'on catchyoo" and is the equivalent of "Gotcha!")

Then they just throw her in the car and haul her off to their mommer'n'em's house and keep her there inside until the sun goes down, after which time she is forevermore "tainted"—as in "used goods" or "no longer a girl" or "crumpled rose" or "former virgin"—and no other man will want her, so she might as well go on and marry the guy on the spot. During this holding period (otherwise known as the "engagement" or "betrothal") the whole gang—friends, Mom and Dad, all the relatives—work in concert to try to throw a white shawl over the head of the fiancée, which, if they're successful, represents her "submission." Some of the potential brides are anything *but* submissive. Some of 'em are downright unruly and manage to thrash the groom and a good many of his kinfolk in the fray.

This business has been going on for *centuries* over there, and somehow we are just now hearing about it. A big selling point, as far as the guys over there are concerned, is the economy of the whole deal. I mean, think of how much money they save! In this part of the world, dating is just a *huge* financial drain. Suppose you date somebody for a year before marriage and you have two dates a week; by the time you add up the entertainment costs and gasoline, and throw in mandatory gifts for Christmas, birthday, and Valentine's, it's easily a ten-thousand-dollar proposition—not counting haircuts and dry-cleaning or even *thinking* about the mental wear and tear.

In this particular vowel-poor country, a basic bride will cost

you about eight hundred dollars plus a cow. I know about a million guys—grooms and dads alike—who'd take that deal all day
long. That right there sounds like the bargain of the century in
dollars alone. When you add in the time and *bullshit* savings,
well, it becomes downright irresistible.

I do love analogies from the animal kingdom, and our In-House
Frog Genius Queen, Carol—sister of one of our preeminent
SPQ Wannabes, Cecilia—shared with me some pertinent facts
about frog fucking, which may be beneficial to us all. (Let us
hasten to clarify that we are referring to an act done *by* frogs,
not *with* frogs, an activity deemed most UnQueenly.)

In late winter a whole bunch of boy frogs will gang up at a
water hole and start bellowing to attract girl frogs. (Queen Carol
questions the potential effectiveness of this tactic for the human
race. What if a bunch of guys got together and just started hollering at the top of their lungs that there was a really great sex-
ual opportunity *right here* for any interested females? Sounds
like any bar I've ever been in, actually.) Apparently, female frogs
think this is a swell way to choose a mate. Good as any, I suppose, love being the crapshoot that it often is.

So anyway, the girl frogs hear the Big Croak, and they all
come a-lookin', and then it all turns into your basic cluster-fuck.
As soon as the females arrive on the scene, the males just go
completely nuts and start grabbin' and humpin' anybody that
comes by. Sometimes they even grab *each other*. (Oh, and I guess

then they say it was an "accident." "Sorry, buddy, thought you were a girl." I am *so sure*.) Anyway, the poor girl frogs get in over their heads, figuratively and literally, and sometimes end up severely injured, if not actually fucked slap to death.

Now, apparently wood frogs are a tad more discerning. The boy wood frogs space themselves in neat little rows around a pool of water and start making these quacking noises. The girl wood frogs come up one by one and look and listen and then decide whose croak is most appealing to them personally, usually based on the frequency and pitch. And they also make their decision based on the frog's size. Bigger is better—seems even frogs know this. This mating game is usually a fairly mannerly proceeding, but we *are* dealing with *guys* here, so every once in a while mistakes do happen. Like, for instance, if this guy frog is sitting there singing his heart out and he's so into his song and all that he kinda tunes out his surroundings but then detects that someone has moved in close to him, well, without so much as an introductory "Hidee!" he just *assumes* it's a willing female and grabs her up in the "mating clasp" (known to frog people as the "amplexus"). But—get this—if it's another guy frog, he will know at once from the *feel*. A desirable female is round and plump, because she's full of eggs. So if he grabs a *skinny* frog, he lets go pretty dang quick, because he knows he's either got hold of a *guy* or a girl that's already mated and released her eggs and is therefore just too skinny to fool with. Now, I like that part right there—don't nobody wanna fool around with no skinny-ass frog girl. "Fat Is Fine" if you're a frog, and I'm hopeful that one day, in my lifetime, big asses will be back in demand for us human folk as well.

Sometimes, Carol tells me, a girl frog will have picked out just the Very One she's after and begin her approach, only to be waylaid (that pun is irresistible!) by "satellite males." These little wimp-bag frogs hang around the big frog's area, hoping to snag the girls as they come in. Some researchers call these guys "gauntlet males" on account of the female may have to fool around with a whole bunch of them before she can get to the Real Prince. Now, isn't *that* just The Truth? She'll persevere until she gets to Mr. Right, though. As usual, we can learn a lot from the animal kingdom.

2

Making a Bride in Just 365 Days

The Sweet Potato Queendom has led to three weddings that I know of. (I haven't kept count of the divorces.) My own wedding, of course. You'll recall that I first met the Cutest Boy in the World at an *SPQ* book event, and he's been following me around ever since. Then, after he'd chased after me for a couple of years, he barged into the hip-hop dance class I was taking and upped and asked me to marry him.

Along about that same time,

I had a book signing in Atlanta, at the Peachtree Battle Chapter 11 to be eggzackt, and who should be standing in line but Mary Kay McCarty and Adam Bridgers. Fortunately, also in the line was Mary Kay's so-smart sister, Monica, who was impressed that Adam was smart and funny enough to buy a *Sweet Potato Queens* book. Since he passed that muster, she checked out his left hand and found it bare, so she struck up a conversation with him, drew her sister, Mary Kay, into it, and split. When she came back an hour later, Monica found Mary Kay and Adam standing outside the store gabbing away. They had their first date the next week and got married thirty months later. All thanks to me. I take full credit—well, I share a little bit with Monica. And they're welcome.

One of the mainmost Queens of the Sweet Potato Queens' Message Board of Love is the very darlin' KimmyDarling. Her equally darlin' boyfriend, Brian, orchestrated a top-secret, super-surprise marriage proposal to her, onstage at the 2004 Sweet Potato Queens' Ball the night before the parade in Jackson. They got married on the beach in Florida that summer.

Not only have some marriages been spawned by the SPQdom, others have been buffed up and restored to like-new luster. I had an intriguing e-mail from a happy-sounding Spud Stud named Mike, who wrote thanking me for jazzing up his marriage to Tammy (her real name, lucky girl). My curiosity piqued, I asked him to please elucidate. He wrote right back, sort of hemming and hawing. I pictured him hanging his head, blushing, scuffing the toe of one shoe, and saying "Aw, shucks" as he answered that, well, they'd both read and liked my books and they'd started taking dancing lessons together and stuff like that and they were having more fun than they'd had since they first met and well, ah . . . they were also having more sex than they'd had since they first got married. "Sincerely, Mike." I did not doubt the sincerity of his note, but if I *had*, it was all dispelled at the legendary Tattered Cover Book Store in Denver, when the very same Mike and Tammy came through my book-signing line. They'd driven eight hours to be there, and they were grinnin' like mules eatin' briars, I gotta tell you. Two *very* satisfied customers, but back to the story line here.

We can't just gloss over that hip-hop class I mentioned earlier, where the Cutest Boy in the World took things into his own hands. Now, this was an absolutely private class—just us Queens and the teacher—held after the rest of the school was shut down, locked down, and otherwise closed for the evening. We went two or three nights a week for I don't know how long, and I gotta tell you: We did *not* learn to hip or hop. We sucked bad. It was utterly demoralizing, especially for TammyMelanie, who is highly competitive and generally highly competent as well, and even *she* couldn't get it. She was not even the least suckee hip-hopper. The truth is, as a group, we were simply unteachable. *We could not get it.* We *did not* get it. We do not *have it*. Hip-hop just plumb eluded our asses.

But we did sweat a lot. And so it was that at the end of one hip-hop class—a particularly dismal night of performance, as I recall, but a spectacular one in the sweating department—the door to our windowless classroom began opening. Someone out there was opening it. This got our attention right away since the building was supposed to be secure against all intruders and observers. As we all turned our sweat-drenched eyes toward the door, who should walk in through it but the cutest little four-year-old blond bombshell of a baby girl you ever saw in your life. It was none other than Olivia Lyons, daughter of our friends Mike and Kelly, who live in Fairhope, Alabama—four hours away. There was no good reason, or even flimsy excuse, for Olivia Lyons to be walking into what I thought was my sealed-off dance class and handing me a bouquet of yellow roses. And then, to further my confusion, strolling in behind her were her parents, toting Olivia's twin siblings, Ethan and Emily, and behind them were Karin and Keifer Wilson, and behind them was TammyCynthia's husband, Joe, and behind him was TammyPippa's husband, Charles, and behind him was my Precious Darlin' George, and behind him was our friend Brewer Pearson, and behind *him* was my mother and my daughter, Bailey. And behind *them* was the Cutest Boy in the World.

And what did the Cutest Boy in the World do but come over and tell me to get up off the floor so that *he could kneel down*. So up I come and down he goes, on one knee. And he's holding out the most gorgeous ring I have ever laid eyes on, and he's asking me if I would do him the very great honor of becoming his wife. And me, I'm snatching that diamond and saying "Uh-huh, buddy" as fast as I can!

Then, with all the Queens standing around, he said he knew better than to think he would just be marrying *me*, and so would they also accept him as my husband? They were pretty quick to chime in affirmatively, too. Of course, they all knew ahead of time; everybody there knew but me. Even the people in the earlier classes who'd been locked out of the building before our class started knew that there was gonna be a marriage proposal that night. But me? I didn't know *nothin'*.

No proposal fantasy I'd ever had in my entire life showed me as an absolute sweat hog in leotards, failing utterly at new dance moves, as the man of my dreams proposes to me in front of all of our friends and family. The group pictures later posted on sweetpotatoqueens.com showed a bunch of clean-looking, happy people (the Cutest Boy in the World, the friends and family) and a bunch of shiny-faced sweat hogs (us). Thank God the Queens didn't come to class all fixed up and cute and then avoid sweating the whole time just so they'd look cute for the photos, leaving *me* the only sweat hog in the group. The payback for that would have been truly frightening.

So anyway, I accepted, began enjoying my big-ass diamond, and looked forward to a long engagement and my year of wedding planning. Because, hunny, to plan a wedding, you're gonna need an entire year—365 days. As you will quickly see, a wedding is a black hole in the universe that's filled with brides from around the world.

My esteemed editor, JoAnne Prichard Morris, questioned whether any woman other than a sweet little larva would spend a whole year planning a wedding. I assured her that it happens all the time. I personally know of one woman, well into her sixties, much denial and plastic surgery to the contrary, who spent an entire year planning the formal wedding of her eighty-something-year-old mother, complete with the groom's great-granddaughter as the flower girl. Any woman—of any age—can lose her mind over a wedding, and that's just the truth.

You will need to *free up all your time* for your year of planning. And when I say free up "all your time," I do mean *all* of it. You should definitely quit your job. There won't be time for it, and the stress can cause unsightly under-eye circles that can be difficult to mask even with the most excellent concealer, and you don't want to spend all your time and money on the Perfect Wedding only to end up looking like a raccoon, now, do you? As soon as you decide that you actually *will* marry a particular person, you should go straight to the Human Resources department at your place of employment and tender your resignation. If you've fooled your employers into thinking that you're a fairly decent employee, they might consider giving you a year's sabbatical for this boondoggle, thinking that once you get the wedding out of your system, you will return and do some actual work again. But under no circumstances will they want to continue your employment during the wedding-planning period. They already know that you won't perform any work-related activities for the duration and that you'll subject everybody else to nonstop discussion and show-and-tell of the entire process, featuring vast quantities of photos. And the HR person wants to slit his or her throat at the very thought of it.

Since you won't be gainfully employed during the wedding-planning process, your best bet is to have parents—birth or adoptive—who are rich as God and nearly as generous, and insist that you quit that pesky job and let them bring over wheelbarrows full of money for your personal use. This is what you'd call your Ideal Situation.

If, on the other hand, your parents don't even have wheel-barrows, let alone money to fill them with, or *if*, let's just say, they have something irritating, like their *own lives*, on which they want to fritter away your rightful wedding funds, then you should have commenced saving your money the very minute you had any vague inkling you might want to have a wedding involving yourself one day far in the future. (Notice I did *not* say that you might have wanted to "get married" one day. Getting married is a negligible expense, but Having a Wedding is another deal altogether.) You should have been collecting cans from the roadsides from the time you could walk. You should have eaten your first-grade paste and hoarded your lunch money. Every time your big sister offered to pay you to leave her and her friends alone, you should have accepted and deposited the bribe in an interest-bearing account. Same with your tooth-fairy earnings. As soon as you were no longer covered under the child-labor laws, you should have been working as many hours as possible and squirreling away every dime, all so you could not only afford the most absurdly extravagant wedding imaginable, but so you'd also be financially able to take at least a year off from work to *plan* the most absurdly extravagant wedding imaginable. It takes that long, at the very least.

Who will pay? All the bridal tutorials I've read put this in the most delicate of terms: "Consult with your fiancé as well as any and all parents to determine the financial support available to you." In other words, who's got what and how much of it can you get hold of? When this is settled, set a budget accordingly. And make sure you include all the activities that could necessitate posting bail for anyone you'll be directly responsible for.

You and your fiancé must decide on the type of wedding you will ultimately, one day in the distant future, actually have. Will it be formal or informal? Large or small? How many people will you have to fool with? This will tell you how big a building you'll need to house this show of dogs and/or ponies. It will be helpful to break the deal down into categories: food, facilities, fashions, and flowers, for instance. And that's only the beginning. You've got to have a photographer *and* a videographer nowadays, as still photos alone won't suffice: We gotta have movies of it all.

Our Precious Darlin' George, who does a bit of wedding work from time to time, says that if you want pictures of *whole* people at your wedding, including your own brideyself, by all means, hire a pro. One bride he assisted was determined to cut at least one corner in the deal, and the one she picked was the photographer. She got her aunt Mary Herschel to take all her wedding photos. (Herschel's not her surname, it's part of her first name. In the South, the first name Mary is likely to be paired with anything and attached to some hapless baby, and then, of course, both names must always be used and it *always* gets slurred and turned into something unrecognizable. This one devolved into "Murhurshel.") Here's something to file away: Once the day is over, it is *over* and you cannot go back and photograph it again. So when Aunt Murhurshel brings over your wedding album or video and it's filled with headless torsos because Aunt Murhurshel is only four-foot-eleven, you'll just have to live with it and spend the rest of your married life trying to identify the bodies.

I've been to celebrations where the hosts put out dozens of disposable cameras and exhort their guests to take scads of what they hope will be great candid shots of all the other guests. This seems like a great idea, unless two of your guests are me and TammyCarol. At our good friend Malcolm White's fiftieth-birthday party, where there were big buckets of disposable cameras, we had a couple of ReVirginators (aka Absolut Fredo—see *The Sweet Potato Queens' Book of Love* or *Big-Ass Cookbook*) and decided that a picture of us with every man at the party would be really cute and highly desirable. Imagine Malcolm's surprise—and, *we* like to think, delight—when he perused his birthday party photos and found shots of me and TammyCarol grinning like a couple of ReVirginated possums with each and every man at the party. From all photographic appearances, we were the only female guests at the entire party, which would account in part at least for the exuberant grinning. (At Malcolm's next big wingding, he personally handed the cameras to carefully selected trustworthy individuals with explicit instructions to photograph as many *different* partygoers as possible and also to be on the lookout for me and TammyCarol trying to insinuate ourselves excessively into the shots.)

Back to the budget. You've got to have music. You've got to have limos. You've got to have hotel rooms and all varieties of auxiliary activities for out-of-town attendees. You've got to have presents for everybody in the wedding party. You've got to have invitations. And don't forget bartenders, candles, champagne, and yes, tips and taxes! You think the preacher or judge will work for free? My God, aren't you out of the mood *yet?*

Fairy~Tale Wedding

Once upon a time, the Cutest Boy in the World was thinking of going to medical school. He consulted with his very wise uncle, Dr. Mark Jumper, and he received this sage advice: "You can go to medical school and work your ass off the entire time and have no personal life whatsoever and be at the very top of your class, and when you graduate, they'll call you Dr. Jennings. [The Cutest Boy in the World's last name is Jennings.] Or you can go to medical school and work juuuust hard enough to get by and have a pret-ty good time of it and barely make it through, and when you graduate, they'll call you Dr. Jennings." Not too comforting a thought for those of us at the mercy of the medical profession, I admit, but that's not the point here. My point is that you can spend all the money in the world and alienate everybody you claim to hold dear. Or you can get our very own Jay Sones, who cleverly ordered off for one of those minister-by-mail certificates, to marry you. Either way, you won't be any *more*—or any *less*—married, and you'll live just as happily ever after. Or not.

3

Choosing the Time and Place

O kay let's start the countdown. We're assuming (read: hoping and praying) that you've Been Particular in your groom selection, that he is perfect for you in every way, and that an acceptable (large) ring has been procured and proffered. So you've got the guy and ring in hand. The first two items to settle on for the wedding are the date and the location, which are often connected. Then we'll work backward from there with a veritable mountain of mindless details that will confound you with their utter insignificance once the wedding year has come and gone and you are no longer the bride. You are merely a wife and you are married to that husband.

As soon as I got my big-ass diamond from the Cutest Boy in the World, the Queens began figuring out where and when we would be marrying. Everyone was heavily invested in this wedding. TammyCynthia was determined that we would have the wedding outside at her beautiful lake house. This was mainly because some guys who owned a big-ass tent company owed her a favor, and she figured our wedding was as good an excuse as any to have a big-ass party with one of their tents. Then there was TammyMelanie, who wanted a lake wedding because she was eager to perform a spectacular Cypress Gardens–type water-skiing act. (She claimed that her "troupe," the Coochie Sprangs Skiers, could form a pyramid on skis.) TammyCarol just hoped there'd be occasion to use her bullhorn. The Tammys Annelle, Donna, Pippa, and Sylvia—and George—really only cared about what *their* wedding outfits were gonna be. Naturally. So they were just pushing for a decision, any decision, so we could get to the good part.

So we decided on a lakeside wedding and set the date. May, it would be. *But*—and it was a very *big* but—at the time, the Cutest Boy in the World and I were working on a pilot for a sit-com based on the Sweet Potato Queens for the WB Network. The L.A. crowd was just oh so thrilled about our engagement until we said the wedding would be in May. This news did *not* thrill them. As a matter of fact, they expressly forbade us to get married in May. (As if we were down here awaiting a dispensation from them.) According to them, if the pilot did get picked up—and we certainly hoped it would—all manner of stuff would hit the fan in the month of May. We never understood what the May stuff would be, but we could tell they were sincerely worried that we were going to screw it up with our silly *wedding.* So we said fine, we'd just pick another time. No big deal. How hard could *that* be?

Well, it turned out to be pretty danged hard. We started out in September with the official engagement, and it was the end of November when the folks in Hollywood made their pronouncement, barring us from a May marriage. I was leaving for a two-month book tour the first week in January, and when I got back, it would be nearly St. Paddy's Parade time. By the time I recovered from the Million Queen March, it would be practically May. So all of a sudden, what we were left with was getting married within the next six weeks or living in sin for an undetermined amount of time, which was not altogether unappealing, but we were just in a marryin' state of mind. We pushed the date back as far as we could and came up with December 31—New Year's Eve, it would be.

The date. So much to consider. Depending on where you live and the nature of the potential groom, you'll have to allow for various hunting seasons and assorted sports seasons (except for NASCAR—it's universal and allthedamntime). When fall rolls around in the South, Saturday is known to be College Football Day—all day, and it doesn't matter just a whole big lot whether or not "your" team is playing. And Friday is for traveling to the away games or attending high-school football, while Sunday is for recovering from all the partying and making the return trip. Sunday's also *Pro* Football Day, and so you've got your Saints and your Cowboys to worry about, and you've got to keep up with Eli *and* Peyton Manning. So you can see that fall weekends are really inconvenient times to have Southern weddings.

Queen Ashley, who lives in Shreveport, Louisiana, was marrying—or attempting to marry—an LSU fan on a Saturday in the fall. Smack in the middle of the ceremony, which was, in Ashley's words, "just as big and Catholic as it could have been," as they're kneeling at the altar in front of the priest and the entire congregation, the groom leans over and whispers to her, "You know, I *am* missing the LSU-Georgia game . . . for this." I'm surprised she didn't earn a "clipping" or even an "unnecessary roughness" penalty after she heard that. Boy, is *he* lucky. But then, under the circumstances, I suppose *she* was lucky he even showed up. He could have insisted they get married at halftime.

Not only do you have to select a time and day when you can reasonably expect the groom to attend, but a time when he'll halfway pay attention to the proceedings. You don't want anyone to have the slightest excuse for distraction or out-and-out absenteeism. After the year you're going to put into planning this thing, you damn sure want everybody and their grandmother there to see it and pay attention.

Potential weather conditions are also important to consider in regards to the date as well as to the location. Winter is pretty much out everywhere north of Key West—it will either be snowing or raining. If you happen to be a white girl, you will be at your absolute whitest then, too, and this doesn't offer much contrast between you and your outfit, assuming you're wearing white—and, of course, you are. Tanning beds will kill you, but more important, they'll kill your skin first. I don't care how you dress it up; beef jerky just does not look virginal. Spray-on tan is safe enough, but unless you do it *eggzackly* right, the spray and drip patterns will have you looking sort of tortoiseshell; plus, it will sweat off on your snow-white gown and look unspeakably nasty.

And then there's summer, which is a really hot time to be wearing that big-ass dress—best be thinking about *that*, too, missy. If you have curly hair but have succumbed to the recurring fad of ironing it to a surreal state of board-straightness, you need to factor in the humidity potential, which renders timing in the South totally moot. It's *always* too humid here, and you'll be needing to relocate the event to Arizona. Down here, we also have many months during which we are entirely likely to have a big giant hurricane that can just blow the whole thing, quite literally. Hurricanes remind me of my friend Chalmers. One day I drove up to see him and found him and his plumber buddy, Steve, underneath the house. Apparently, Chalmers' skill was insufficient in Steve's eyes because what I heard blasting out of the vents in the foundation was Steve's almost-helium-high-pitched rant: "Goddammit, Chalmers, you're just like a monkey: What you don't fuck up, you shit on!" And that's kinda what I think about hurricanes in the South. Not conducive to wedding day perfection a-tall.

You need to somehow arrive at a mutually agreeable date, and then have at least three alternate dates on account of the odds of both sets of relatives being willing and available for your wedding on the very first day you throw out there—well, they're just slim and none, is all. But do try real hard to keep in mind that really only two people absolutely *have* to be at your wedding, and that would be the two of y'all. Most of the others you're trying to arrange your life around would just as soon go bowling.

Auxiliary Dates of Importance

Once you have the wedding date settled, it's time to plan for the Announcement Party, which according to my source Lynda Wright, is the new Reception. (You may remember Lynda from a previous book as the woman whose Ultimate Tool for Avoiding Any and All Things She Doesn't Want to Fool With is to say in her so-Southern drawl that she would love to, but she just had her eyes dilated.) The Wedding Announcement Party has taken on such *great* pith and import that "getting" to give this party is a privilege much wrangled over. I myself cannot imagine such a thing. I'm so lazy, I can scarcely get around to attending parties, much less *having* them—and for other people, to boot. I am agog.

Choosing the Time and Place

Perusing the society sections of our local news publications, I see that Lynda is much in the know on this subject. There are features on the Wedding Announcement Parties of dozens of different couples with their smiling, sweaty-looking well-wishers in attendance. (Not sweaty-looking as if they'd been working in the yard, now, just kind of damp and shiny from eating and drinking to somewhat over the level of excess.) My sister, Judy (Judy Conner, author of *Southern Fried Divorce*, Gotham Books, 2005), and I love to read these because they're very descriptive in the areas of most interest to us: what everybody had on and what all they had to eat. We can devour entire books consisting of little more than exhaustive details about clothing and food.

Queen Denise, who describes herself and her friends affectionately as "Coonasses"—also known as "Cajuns" in south Louisiana—said she went to a party for a couple of engaged Coonasses where they served whole *lunch meat* sandwiches, crust and all. I'm sorry, but that would be called a "sammich" where I come from. I confess, I was shocked. Cajuns are famous for their feeds—entire pigs are roasted regularly and no crawfish is safe. I didn't know they even had lunch meat in south Louisiana. It must have been imported from somewhere in the Midwest, where I think it grows on trees. If this is what's passing for nouveau cuisine in Cajun Country, it's a sad day indeed. Until Emeril has a lunch meat show, though, I'm gonna believe this party food was an aberration.

By far the worst offense to date was described to me by Queen Susan from College Station, Texas. She was invited to an

Announcement Party cookout, and the invitations instructed guests to "bring your own meat for grilling." A very large grill would be on hand, the invite said, and "if you want to eat—bring some meat." The mental picture forms of the arriving guests clutching assorted hunks of cow and pig, the lawn littered with bloody butcher paper and Styrofoam packaging. Once the grilling got under way, quarrels were bound to spring up over which meat belonged to whom. This party was clearly destined to be one of those affairs you read about in the newspaper, with an account that begins, "Among the injured were . . ."

Location, Location, Location

Now, if it's an indoor wedding you want, you're home free. If, however, you decide to do this deal outdoors, you need to be considering some major issues—like relocating to a more temperate clime, dealing with mosquitoes, and don't forget fire ants. I don't know if y'all have these things where you live, but lemme tell you something: You do not want to fight with fire ants. They nearly *always* win and they do not fight fair. They can kill you— quite literally—and they want to, real bad.

I know of one hapless bride who wasn't even trying to have an outdoor wedding—the whole thing was inside a church with good air-conditioning and everything. But she had to come in from the back of the sanctuary, which meant she was standing outside on the sidewalk for a few minutes. It was a nice enough day and she wasn't sweating or anything, and the wind wasn't messing her hair up. She was just real happy standing out there, looking all bridey and smiling and waving at the folks driving by and talking to her daddy, who was trying not to cry. Presently, she heard the "dum-dum-de-dum's" starting in the sanctuary, and so she and her daddy went up the steps into the church.

Well, about halfway down the aisle, she started screaming and flailing at herself, hiking her dress up and swatting at her legs with her bouquet and carrying on in a complete "mad-bride-ish" kinda way. Then her daddy chimed in: *He* started hollering and slapping and clawing at *him*self and hopping around. The people seated next to the aisles were leaning way away from the pair. Whatever it was that had got hold of the wedding party, they didn't want none of it gettin' on *them*. The organist just kept right on "dum-dum-de-dum-ing," completely oblivious to the fact that the whole entire wedding had just gone to shit in the middle of the center aisle of the church. Nobody could get anywhere near the duo to see what the problem was, and they were hollering too much and too loud for anybody to ask what the problem was. Everybody in attendance was just pretty much spellbound, as you may imagine.

The screaming and thrashing went on for what seemed like forever to participants and spectators alike, but by and by, a keen-eyed observer discerned the problem: fire ants. When Bride and Daddy were standing outside the church waiting to come in, they had unwittingly stood in a fire-ant crossing, and the ants had been forced to take a detour up that big fancy wedding dress and tuxedo. There'd apparently been a big turnout that day for some kind of fire-ant festivity because Bride and Daddy were pretty much covered from the feet up in fire ants and fire-ant bites.

The preacher finally got the organist to quit playing. As the murmured echoes of "Fire ants!" rippled across the congregation, the infested duo were herded through the church to their respective restrooms and stripped naked by friends and loved ones, who were also bitten for their efforts (by the ants, not the bride and Daddy). The ants were all executed summarily, but the problem was hardly solved. Now you had the most important people in the ceremony naked in the bathrooms and covered in fire-ant bites. If you've never had the experience, I can tell you they itch and sting like proverbial MF'ers. As I said, fire ants can kill you and they want to whenever they can. I think they must win a really swell fire-ant trophy when they do. Anyway, the bride and her daddy were just *runt*. (If you live outside the South, you need to know that word means the same as *ruined*, but you gotta agree, it sounds way worse.) They were pure-dee *runt*—both of 'em crying, and no wonder. The folks who'd rescued them were not a whole lot happier.

Fortunately, the allergy-suffering church secretary was willing to share her economy-size box of Benadryl, and those folks were eating them things like candy. Then they had to go take a serious nap—well, after they got out of the emergency room, of course. They just told the guests to go on to the reception and eat and drink and dance and have a big ole time; the wedding itself would take place when the bride could be awake without scratching. So the show did go on, just without the star and a few supporting actors. A few weeks later the preacher married the couple in a family ceremony, which didn't make anywhere near as good a story, and the pictures weren't as entertaining, either.

If any part of your shindig is gonna take place out of doors, do be sure to have the sprinkler system turned O-F-F. Our Head Wannabe, the very Precious and Darlin' George, besides having the very important job of being our chief lackey, is also a landscape architect, floral designer, caterer, wedding coordinator, and party planner. At a moment's notice, George can re-create the Rain Forest Café at Disney World out of the stuff he routinely rides around with in his Jeep. Anyway, George was handling an outdoor wedding once, and right before the bride came out, the entire yard erupted into Old Faithful. He and his faithful minions, having no earthly idea where the sprinkler controls were located, let alone how to reprogram them once they'd begun their rain cycle, ran through the church kitchen and snatched up every single pot and pan and then tore through the churchyard, clapping a makeshift cover over each spigot. Sounded like the bride was being pursued by a large swarm of bees, but, thank goodness, she was dry.

George told me about another posh Mississippi Delta wedding with an outdoor reception planned, where at the end of the ceremony the preacher instructed everybody to go on home and "put on your grubbies—it's been rainin' for two whole days and there's no sign of it lettin' up now." George was amused to see the always-so-refined and dignified television talk-show host Dick Cavett in attendance—in a three-piece suit, with knee-high rubber boots.

And if you're gonna commit matrimony outside, do take into consideration the possibility of active participation by live-stock. Not that you should try to incorporate livestock into the ceremony, but you might want to be aware that any, say, cows in the vicinity might just decide on their own, without prior consultation, invitation, or encouragement of any kind, to insin-uate themselves into the situation. Queen Allison Lowery Fuller (she prefers to use her whole title) told me that her cousin got married on the front porch of their aunt Louise's house, one of those big ole North Carolina plantation affairs, which sits right next to a large pasture filled with cows. It was August and hot as the hammered-down hinges of hell, and everybody was sweatin' and standin' around waiting for the thing to begin—so it could be over, I'm sure, and they could go inside and cool off. They all were so relieved when the wedding singer began trilling in her very high soprano voice—at least there was action—but their relief soon turned to panic. The *cows*, it seems, were quite taken with the very high soprano voice of the wedding singer, or driven mad by it—it was hard to make the distinction—because all of them, in unison, quite suddenly gave voice their ownselves—very loud, bellowing cow-voice. Then en masse (or would it be en herde?), they came thundering up to the fence, a flimsy-looking wire affair, and they pushed and pressed against it, straining to break through, pawing at the ground, the fence, and one another, mooing madly all the while. The upside is no one in the family ever forgets the couple's anniversary.

In some parts of the world, the scene would have been so different. In certain rural areas of Germany, for instance, it's considered bad form *not* to have a cow in the wedding party. I read in the paper, I swear, about a wedding with a cow named Paula, who was the guest of honor. Now, during the ceremony Miss Paula wandered off. Cows apparently do not have the memories attributed to elephants, and Paula forgot that she was an honored guest at a wedding. She did, however, remember that she needed to go to the *bank*, and so she did. She left the ceremony and strolled into a nearby financial institution. The bank spokeswoman reported that it was an extraordinary experience for the banking customers and employees alike, but "it was over very quickly." Paula simply entered the bank and made an "elegant turn." That's what the newspaper said—*the cow made an elegant turn*. (Let me just say no one has ever described any movement of mine in terms anything like "an elegant turn," and perhaps the same is true for you? Guess we could all take a page out of ole Paula's book.)

Anyway, immediately following her elegant turn, Paula vacated the bank, and who knows what happened after that? The newspaper account was not nearly detailed enough about this whole thing. It did, however, tell me that the cow was at the wedding in keeping with local custom. Perhaps she was a cow hired for the occasion rather than a personal family cow for whom the ceremony would've had personal meaning, and that explains her aberrant wedding behavior. Paula was invited to the wedding so the bride—as a part of the ceremony—could *milk* her, thus demonstrating her (the bride's) skills. Now, that right there brings up yet another glaring lapse in the reporting of this event: There was *no mention whatsoever* of the skills the *groom* would or should be called upon to demonstrate.

I'm not sure about other parts of the country, but in the South, the cow is actually the impetus for a large number of weddings each year. Those of us of a Certain Age do recall our mamas' admonitions against fooling around with boys to whom we were not officially married. It went like this: "Why should he buy the cow when he gets the milk for free?!" As I have grown much older, I've examined this cow maxim and found it somewhat flawed. The unmistakable implication of the statement is that once one *owns* the cow, the milk is then free. Well, har-de-har-har is all I can say to that. Clearly this little axiom was coined by some igmo who'd never in his life been married *or* owned livestock, since both propositions are among the most costly undertakings imaginable.

Wives and cows alike can exact heavy tolls—pain, money, heartache, and tears—you name it. Ask anybody who's ever had either one—or worse, both! Certainly *free* is not a term that pops up often in discussions about marriage or cattle. (I personally do wonder, though, how come nobody ever raised the question of "Why should *we* buy the *pig* when all we want is a little sausage?")

Themes

Whether the wedding is outdoors or in, there are those who actually believe that a regular wedding is not enough trouble; they need a special theme. Now, before you get into that, missy, you need to sit down with a cup of coffee and go back through a few photo albums and look at stuff you wore in public, say, five or ten years ago that seemed like such a good idea at the time. Pay close attention to the coffee spurting spontaneously out through your nostrils as you gaze with hilarious horror at your former self. Is that the experience you want to relive every time you look at your wedding photos for the rest of your life?

I've seen it where the "theme" was carried out only in the *food* at the reception. For example, one couple I know first met and fell in love while they were performing in a community theater production of *You're a Good Man, Charlie Brown.* He was Charlie Brown and, naturally, she was The Little Red-Haired Girl. Awwwww. So, of course, at the reception, they felt like they just *had* to have this big giant Charlie Brown made entirely of cheese. It was clearly disturbing to see his body disappear, bit by bit, onto crackers and into the smacking mouths of the wedding guests.

Even more disturbing, I heard from someone who attended a wedding where there was a Disney theme for everybody in the wedding. Yup. And everybody got to choose his or her own Disney character! The bride was Cinderella. All your favorites were there, of course, and somewhere in the wedding party there was even a Grumpy Dwarf. I don't know if the groom was assigned to be the prerequisite Prince Charming or if, left to his own devices, he showed up for the day as Goofy.

Me, I think the best thing is to figure out some way to go out in public and flounce around in your very fancy big white dress. It's the only time you get to wear it, after all, and you want as many people as possible to see you in it. Queen Viv of the Sweet Potato Queens Message Board of Love and her Precious were having a big Halloween party. They'd secretly gotten married that morning and came to their own costume party in their very fine wedding attire—Precious in his tux, Viv in the big white dress. After they won "Best Costumes" (at their own costume party!), they announced to the decked-out guests that it was for real: They had gotten hitched that very morning. A drunk in a pirate outfit with a stuffed parrot on his shoulder gave Viv a large congratulatory thump, causing her full glass of cabernet to cascade in a ruby torrent down the front of the big white dress. Okay, so you want as many people as possible to *see* you in the big white dress, but you don't want them to be able to get at you.

One of my favorite Spud Studs, Charles, told me he once attended a wedding where there was a "mini bride." Now, let's just stop and visualize *that* for a minute or two. I can't decide which aspect of that horrifies me the most. First, there's the whole competition-with-the-bride issue. Little girls are bad to compete for attention anyway, but put one of 'em in a big, fancy bride's dress and trot her out to perform in front of a church full of people, and just try and get her to give up center stage. Good *luck*, buckwheat. And then, too, there's the whole creep-factor thing about dressing little girls up in really inappropriate grown-up-girl outfits. I don't wanna see 'em dressed like Britney Spears, *either.* Too much too soon. And too icky in the meantime.

Anyway, Charles said he saw the mini bride and he suggested another nice touch would be to have a *maxi* bride as well. I did think that was pretty hilarious, and he said he even had a wedding dress he could donate for such an occasion if we were interested. An ex of his had worn it—only once—and even that was a mistake! He allowed as how the wearer would need to have large "lungs" to hold it up. If we decided we didn't want it, though, he thought he'd make a throw net out of it and go shrimping. Way to recycle there, Charlie-boy!

4

Big Juju Dresses

O key-dokey. At least a year in advance of
the ceremony, you get the supreme
shopping pleasure of commencing the
all-important Bride's Dress Selection.
I'm quite sure that a *goodly* number of
you, like me and some of my nearest
and dearest, have gone into a bridal shop
and taken turns trying on big-ass wedding dresses when not a one of you had
so much as a date for the weekend, let
alone a fiancé. Don't be embarrassed—
we've all done it. It's genetic and irresistible. But now that you're
actually in possession of a suitable fiancé (well, only time will

tell how "suitable" he is, but he's in the bag at the moment, so fine), it's time for some bona fide bridal shoppage. You have several options available to you, ranging from the Internet (nah, 99 percent of the fun is trying them all on with your best girlfriends) to your wedding party outfitter chains (excellent for bargains). Then there are your chichi ultra-exclusive bridal *salons*, where you pretty much gotta dress up even to go in, and no matter how stunningly you're dressed, the staff will look at you with a mixture of pity and amusement, with just a smidgen of disgust for good measure. (I'm sure these women were the genesis of Princess Diana's much-lamented eating disorder.) Then you've got your rental establishments, of course. And then there's my very favorite place to shop for just about *anything* wedding-related, on account of they *got* it, as evidenced by their sign, which reads WILLIE STEVE'S ONE-STOP—GUNS—WEDDING GOWNS—COLD BEER. Willie Steve is quite the forward-thinking entrepreneur, in my opinion. (My fellow author Cassandra King and I have made a hobby of finding hilarious store signs. Some of the best ones in my collection are WIGS—PECANS—SCRAP METAL and MOBILE HOMES—BOAT STORAGE—POLLED HEREFORDS. My favorite ladies' shop is aptly named Dressin' Gaudy, and to date, my all-time-favorite establishment offers the following wide range of services: CHILD EVANGELISM—EYEGLASS REPAIR. I swear to God. Do you really think I could make this shit up?) Anyway, you've got lots of options, and for the full Bridal Experience, you need a number of widely varied shopping excursions.

The first and most important consideration is that you shop at the actual time of day when your wedding will eventually be held. The reason, of course, is that you need to try on dresses at the appropriate time for your *body*. Nobody hardly ever gets married at 6:30 A.M.—that's 6:30 *in the morning*—and it's a damn shame, because that's about the best your body is gonna look all day. Your face and head may look like you just hopped outta bed and chased a fart through a keg of nails, but your *body* will be as good as it will get, since you haven't had time to swell up yet. When those somewhat older British women made that nekkid calendar of themselves, all the photos were shot in the early morning for that very reason.

On the other hand, if you plan to get married when most humans are up and willing to attend functions, well, by that late in the day, you will be blown up like a big bowl of bread dough on its second rising, and the dress you select will need to be prepared to accommodate All That Is You. So you'll want to schedule your shopping trips for after lunch. I think this is an excellent plan, anyway, so you and your girlfriends can fortify yourselves with a sumptuous repast before the rigorous hunt begins. My sister, Judy, and I have always liked to schedule *all* our daily activities around as many meals as we can possibly squeeze in, which makes for lots of good eatin' without leaving much time for a whole big lot of errand runnin'—just the way we like it. Plan your food first and then, *if time permits*, slip in an activity here and/or there. We do just hate to eat in a hurry, don't you?

Big Juju Dresses

Say there, how do you feel about relocating to Nigeria? Run it past that fiancé of yours and see what he thinks. Over in Nigeria they apparently just *looooove* fat brides. In fact, fat women are practically worshipped over there for any occasion—what a lovely sentiment: I ♥ NIGERIA! I'm thinking that is just the place I wanna grow old and fat—okay, fatter—in. They even have special farms they ship prospective brides off to—fat farms, if you will, but with a decidedly better connotation than the ones we have over here, in my opinion. Yes, indeedy-do, if you are officially engaged over there, you get trotted off to a special fat-bride farm where they feed you all manner of fattening stuff round the clock. And then they *massage* your body into even *more* roundness. It's kinda like being Kobe beef in a bride's dress. (You know, the cows they make Kobe beef out of never have to lift a hoof. They are fed the very best grain and *beer* around the clock and get rubbed on constantly to keep 'em tender. Of course, it almost *never* ends well for these cows—but then, the whole marriage thing is pretty risky its ownself, I reckon.) If this is not heaven, I just don't know what is, is all I'm saying. I predict that after the publication of this book there'll be a huge surge in Nigeria's immigrant population, mostly from the States, and furthermore, that Nigerian men in the U.S.A, never lacking in popularity, will no longer be able to walk safely down the streets without being accosted by the plump.

Some days, mostly the ones when I look in the mirror, I'm wishing I had me a nice fat-worshipping Nigerian husband instead of the Cutest Boy in the World, who—did I tell you?—

lost twenty pounds, without trying or exercising. (And he's kept them off without trying or exercising.) He didn't have them to lose, and I, of course, *found* every one of them. I mean, he is cute and all that, but if that is not grounds for justifiable homicide, I just don't know what is.

But I digress. Back to the dress hunt. I have a fair amount of varied experience in this area. When I was a wee, young thing—well, that's a lie; I never had a "wee" day in my life, but I was young for a little while a long, long time ago, and back then, I had me a wedding with the ineffable Ray-boy. We had differing views on the whole deal. I wanted small and simple; he wanted big and fancy. I wanted to wear something by Jessica Somebody-or-other, who made dresses that looked like they might have been fashioned out of gunnysacks. Their appeal was pretty universal—we all loved her stuff. We were pseudo-quasi-semi-wannabe hippies, I guess. Anyway, Ray-boy wanted to wear a tux and *tails* even. I nixed the tails but said he could wear a tux if he was panicking to, but I was wearing a gunnysack number. Well, that was my plan *until* I went to the Bridal Shoppe. (Just the fact that they had two *p*'s and a gratuitous *e* in their name tells it all, I think.) And yes, they did have a Jessica Somebody-orother dress for me to try on—fashioned from a coarse, unbleached fabric and very hip—and, oh, did I love it! Mother's lips were pressed together in a painful little line as she looked balefully at the dress consultant, who understood completely. Apparently, our bridal lady had been going through this with all the young pseudo-quasi-semi-wannabe hippie brides that year.

You know, it was Mississippi in the early seventies, and we wanted *so bad* to be so hip and cool, but, you know, it was Mississippi in the early seventies. Nobody had really been very far from home for very long at a time or had more than two thoughts of their own yet. We had heard that hipness was out there and we knew we wanted it *bad*, but that's about as far as it went.

The dress consultant was no dummy. She'd seen this coming and had that requisite Jessica Somebodyorother dress just a-hangin' there for all of us who strolled in and spoke in tones dripping knowledge of the cool and dropping that name so offhandedly: "Oh, do you have any Jessica Somebody-or-other? I'd like to try her, please." And she—if she was smirking, she hid it well—would trot off and fetch the requested dress. And the young pseudo-quasi-semi-wannabe hippie brides would all adore it: It was just the vision we'd been dreaming of, ourselves in the gunnysack dress, long hair down and parted in the middle, barefoot*ed* (nobody goes "barefoot" down here), taking our vows in the meadow with the barefooted groom and the barefooted minister, in front of the very hip gathering of our very hip barefooted friends. I'm not sure how we thought all the shoe-wearing *parents* were going to fit into this scenario, but it was, after all, only a fantasy—and a short-lived one at that, because while we'd been gazing, mesmerized, at our own hip reflection in the gunnysack, the dress consultant had exchanged A Look with our mother, and before we suspected the conspiracy, our dressing room was filled with unspeakably gorgeous creations of silk and chiffon and embroidery and lace. We-e-e-elll, it wouldn't hurt to just *try on* one or two of 'em after she went to all the trouble of haulin' 'em in here and all—wouldn't want to hurt her feelings or anything.

I swear, I wonder sometimes at just what all Southerners will do in the course of a day in the name of Not Hurting Somebody or Other's Feelings. I remember once, sitting at a traffic light behind a bunch of cars and seeing this lunatic loose amidst the traffic, running, wild-eyed, up to cars and yelling unintelligibly, while rending his hair and clothing in a most distressing manner. Later on I recounted my experience to my daddy and told him I was so afraid the crazy guy would get to my car before the light changed because, since my doors weren't locked, I'd have to reach up and lock 'em, right in front of him and thereby run the risk of *hurting his feelings!* When Daddy repeated it back to me—"You didn't want to hurt the crazy guy's feelings by locking your doors in front of *him?*"—it really didn't seem as logical anymore.

Anyway, back in the shoppe, and purely to satisfy my mother and spare the delicate feelings of the Dress Lady, I reached out and touched the first gown—and the juju struck me. It not only struck me square in the face, it crawled all over me and ran up and down my spine like it had little tiny feet in felt slippers. It got inside my head and guts until I felt like I'd swallowed two or three hummingbirds. To say it was all over then wouldn't be quite accurate, because the juju had just gotten started. I tried on the one and that led to the next one and that one to the next one and the next and the next—and so on and on and on. It would be exceedingly accurate, however, to say it was all over for the pseudo-quasi-semi-wannabe *hippie* wedding. Yessireebobtailcat—that vision of hipness was history. My mother resumed breathing at that point. She was going to have a Real Wedding after all, one with shoes and ever'thang.

After several truly exhausting visits to plenty of bridal salons, I settled on an exquisite example of brideliness. It is damn hard to choose, I'll just tell you. Those dresses are some powerful juju—uh-huh, they are. The juju is easy to understand. All you have to do is put *on* one a' those suckers and look in a mirror. *Everybody* looks gorgeous in a wedding dress. No, I'm serious—*everybody*. (I have photos of Our Precious Darlin' George looking gorgeous in a lovely snow-white gown he purchased at Hudson's Salvage Store, and *he* even looks somewhat virginal.) I don't care what physical flaws you have, real or imagined, they all disappear if you put 'em in one a' those dresses. Fairy wand music should spontaneously erupt whenever one is donned; the transformation is that immediate and complete. You stand in the dressing room in your underwear and look in the mirror—ehhhh, dogball, you think to yourself. But on with the big magic dress and literally presto/chango—*boi-oi-oi-oi-oi-oing-nnnnggggng* (fairy wand sound)—one of those oft-touted "visions of loveliness" is looking back at you out of that mirror, and it's *you!* If you come across a more powerful juju than *that*, hunny, buy up all of it you can. Never in the history of the entire world, living or dead, has anybody ever tried on one of those dresses and then decided, Oh, you know, I don't really want all *that*. Oh no, ma'am, that ain't never happened. What does happen *plenty*, though, is just what happened to me: I went *in* thinking, Oh, you know, I don't really want all *that*, only to be waylaid, blindsided, ambushed, and bushwhacked by the Big Juju of the Bride's Dress.

For my *next* wedding, I discovered on a Wednesday that I was pregnant and called all my friends to tell them the happy news and that I would be getting married a week from Friday! My mother was properly horrified that I would tell such a thing. And I just looked at her and said, "You know, Mama, I'm thirty-five years old, and I'm *happy* about this. It's not like I'm twelve and he's my first cousin. I'm happy, and my friends are all *grown-up women* and they love me and they will be happy for me as well." The idea of calling up these women, who know *everything* there is to know about me, and I, them, and laying a bunch of crap on them . . . "Guess *what?!* We're getting *married!* Next Friday—isn't that wild?! Yes, in a *week!* No, no special reason. We just want to get married *as quickly as possible!*" And then, in a few months, looking these same women dead square in the eye and saying, "Oh! Guess *what?!* I'm *pregnant!* We're so *surprised!* No, we're not sure when I'm due—it's too soon to tell!" And then, in a few months, calling these same women (did I mention that they are my best friends in the whole entire world and they know everything about me, and I, them?) and telling them, "Oh! Guess *what?!* I had the baby this morning! Yes, we were *so surprised!* She wasn't due for at least two more months! No, she's just fine—weighed eight pounds! Yes, how lucky she came early.

If she'd gone *full-term*, she'd a weighed twenty-five or thirty pounds!"

"Mama," I wailed, "they're my *best friends*. I can't *lie* to them. I don't *want* to lie to them. *I'm happy*. Just be happy for me. I'm thirty-five, and I thought I'd never get to have a baby!"

So we agreed on a compromise: Mama could lie about it to *her* friends, which, of course, she did. And they all went along with the charade and were just so surprised and happy for me when I got pregnant so soon after my wedding, and they were just as surprised and happy for me when my daughter came so early and yet, luckily, was fully formed and healthy.

Anyway, I didn't opt for the big juju bride's dress for that occasion. Something linen and appropriately understated, as I recall. Mama was pleased, and she was reeeally pleased with the absolutely *perfect* baby girl I managed to produce some months later. Her pleasure with that baby has continued unabated for the last seventeen years and shows no sign of diminishing. (I got *that* part right, anyway, huh, Mama?)

My *third and final* wedding—this time with the Cutest Boy in the World—was also a rush job, though, sadly, not due to pregnancy. After the hip-hop proposal and date selection ordeal, we had to get into high gear to plan that small, sedate wedding at our small wonderful church, Wells United Methodist, in Jackson. (If you're ever in town on a Sunday, you should make the time to go. It's not like any church you've ever seen before, and I mean that in the absolute *best* way. It's the *only* church I've personally attended where *everybody* really is *truly* welcome.)

Then, once things were under way, I could get to the big

issue: my bridal attire. Being six-foot-one and not svelte, I am handicapped in the clothes-shopping arena, as in I can't buy anything but *shoes* to fit me, and that's no picnic, either. If I had long, fat feet, I could buy shoes, cheap, all day long, but keeping long, skinny feet shod costs a bleeding fortune. Now, if I was a size *zero* like my daughter, Bailey, that would be another matter altogether. *She* can walk into any store anywhere, put on anything in a zero or a two, and walk out looking like *Vogue*'s wet dream. The clothes in *my size* are *Vogue*'s worst nightmare; the vision of me *in* them would render *Vogue* sleepless forevermore.

When it was time to shop for my dress, I happened to be in Dallas, speaking at a Junior League event. (For some reason, the Junior Leagues love me, and they've been so very supportive of me that they are the only group for whom I discount my speaker's fee. They love me and I love 'em right back!) After the Junior League event, there was a giant reception at this big fancy mall. I'm thinking, Yippee, I can go in Neiman Marcus and maybe find something not too bridey that I could get married in. But, of course, none of the stores were open, and I was nursing a glass of wine, grousing about that fact on the sidelines, and who should overhear me but the very *manager* of Neiman's herownself. She offered to open up the store on the spot, but I thanked her and declined. This was a big party in her mall and I didn't want to take her away from it. She gave me her card and the phone numbers of the folks who'd be arriving early the next morning to open up; she told me to call 'em up, use her name, and they would let me and my daughter in to shop before the store opened. Can you just imagine the *glee* with which my then-thirteen-year-old daughter greeted the news that we'd be having a private shopping moment in Neiman Marcus? An audience with the pope would've been chump change in comparison. I was pretty pleased about the deal myownself.

The next morning, we got up early, called the secret number, and received our instructions for gaining entry. The Cutest Boy in the World toted us over there, and then he trotted off to "church," the Home Depot across the street. Bailey and I were treated like the Queens we are, and we *both* found excellent wedding garments. When we finished our shopping adventure, we discovered that the Cutest Boy in the World was upstairs in the lovely Neiman's restaurant enjoying complimentary beers and lunch. It was an altogether satisfactory day at the mall, I gotta tell you.

That was for my *serious* wedding clothes—you know, the ones for the actual ceremony, where we would dress appropriately. We both found just what we were looking for that day. I wore ivory crepe pants and an ivory beaded top. Bailey wore black crepe pants and an ivory silk top. *All* of the Queens—they walked me down the aisle and gave me away, since my daddy's dead—wore black-and-ivory silk pants outfits, designed by our very own TammyDonna. My Precious Darlin' George, who also helped give me away, wore a black suit—even though he *would* have looked lovely in one of the Donna outfits. The Cutest Boy in the World and his daddy also wore black suits. We all looked lovely.

And our invited guests were also especially spiffy-looking.

One of our very dearest friends, who shall remain nameless for reasons that will be obvious in a moment, strode in wearing a striking black-and-ivory suit with the most adorable red hat perched on her stylishly coiffed head. She just pranced herself down the aisle, speaking to one and all, creating quite a stir. All the Queens were cloistered with me in the "cry" room at the back of the church, so we could see everything through the window, and it was quite a sight, believe you me. Little Miss Red Hat had somehow contrived, unbeknownst to herowncuteself, to completely free up her left breast from the constraints of the striking black-and-ivory suit. I'm not talking *bra* here but actual flesh-and-blood bosom—complete with nipplage—just right out there, in the middle of the church. Now, this was way worse than somebody having their fly open or spinach in their teeth. Her bare *tit* was just sitting there, *winking* at the other guests in that brazen manner tits can adopt when you whip them out in unlikely locations. Fortunately for Little Miss Red Hat, she does have very cute and extremely perky tits, so everybody was quite happy to see this one. But it was, after all, the *sanctuary*. Of equal good fortune was the fact that the "cry" room was sound-proof, because the whooping and snorting issuing forth was hardly befitting the decorum of the pre-wedding situation we found ourselves in. We were *moosing* we were laughing so hard, and *nobody* was telling her as she continued to prance about, thinking, no doubt, that everybody was just so taken with her little red hat. Finally we banged on the glass of the "cry" room window and she turned around to see us all flailing around, laughing so hard we cried most of our makeup off, and then we, as a group, acted out for her that she needed to stow that thing away. A lesser woman would have been mortified, but not our Little Miss Red Hat. She merely glanced down and, laughing her lilting laugh, tucked it safely back inside and went right on with her prancing and greeting. Up until that moment, she had known better than anyone just how cute her tits were—but now they all knew, too, and she was not unproud.

I don't think we even have to say that Little Miss Red Hat is not now nor is she ever likely to be connected in any way, shape, or form to the Red Hat Society. If anybody ever mistook her cute little red hat for a badge of membership in that group, she would snatch it from her head and stomp it into the dirt. Her driver's license may say "Fifty-plus" but everything about her screams "Nineteen!" or at the very most "Twenty-seven!" If she lives to be 150, she'll still be too young to be a Red-Hatter.

Bridal Nekkidity

Weddings are generally thought to be—and I think rightfully so—fairly solemn affairs. What goes on with your guests is one thing; what happens with the bride is another matter altogether. Even if you're not doing the deal in a church or temple, the ceremony itself is still pretty dang serious. (You may not realize just *how* serious until you get to the other half of this book.) As such, I think a certain amount of decorum is expected, and this should be reflected nowhere so much as in the neckline of your dress.

By that I mean try to wait until after the completion of the ceremony to whip your tits out.

George reported that the bride in a wedding he handled
recently was just a deep breath away from getting arrested for
indecent exposure in a church. One good sigh would have
sprung her *en*tire bosom, nipples and all, smack out in the middle of the room. The part he could see of them was bigger 'n'
her head, he said, even with the veil. And the way they jiggled
and undulated as she walked down the aisle was nothing short
of mesmerizing to the whole congregation.

Word to the wise: You do not want your wedding to be
remembered by the size of the betting pool on whether or not
your tits will stay in your dress for the whole ceremony. As one
very astute woman advised: Never heave your bosom in a front-
hook bra.

Wardrobe Adjustments

Since we were being cheated out of our lakeside May wedding
at TammyCynthia's house, complete with TammyMelanie's
Cypress Gardens–style water-skiing extravaganza, we needed to
compensate for this deprivation. So we decided that for the
reception, wardrobe changes would be in order.

I myownself was craving something in the giant meringue
order, and the Queens were bad wanting some tacky bridesmaids dresses. When you get as old as we are, the chances for
big-ass white wedding dresses and tacky bridesmaids getups

have become few and far between, and we meant to avail ourselves of this rare opportunity. And so it was that Tammy-
Cynthia and TammyMelanie accompanied me to David's Bridal
(I always wondered just who this David is and what's his obses-
sion with brides), and we fell up in there, carrying on something
awful. You'da thought we were little twentysomething first-
timers. I gave them specific instructions as we began the hunt
for my dress: It had to be pure-as-the-unsullied-snow white and
there was no train too long, no pouf too big. Sing to me of sweet-
heart necklines and sculpted waistlines. Pile on the pearls, enfold
me in embroidery, bring on the bustles, and lavish me with lace.
Let no onlooker doubt that *here* comes the bride. I wanted the
very biggest, most ridiculously inappropriate bridey-looking
thing we could find, and I wanted to buy it cheap, off the rack.
Easy, as I said, if you're a size zero like Bailey. Not so easy for
big giant brides like myownself.

We hauled in every big giant bride's dress ole David had in
stock that day and I stuffed my big giant self into 'em. I had prudently worn the shoes that I planned to be wearing with my big
giant bride's dress—my well-worn Mizuno running shoes. I was,
after all, planning on daincin' at the reception, and as we *all
know*, comfy shoes are the answer to most of life's dilemmas. I
would don each dress, which had clearly been designed with a
teenager in mind, and dutifully model it for the Tammys, who
were acting as my surrogate mom for the occasion. My own
mother was, by this time, *way* past picking out wedding attire
for *my* ass.

There are about fifty dressing rooms at David's, and they were all full of very young and serious brides-to-be, and the viewing area was all full of the even more serious *mothers* of the brides-to-be, and all these mothers appeared to be about our age or younger. They were not entirely appreciative of the high old time we were having. Not appreciative a-tall actually. Nor did they take to it kindly when one of the purported brides came out, squeezed sausagelike into the only remaining dress of a now-discontinued model (naturally, the only one she *really* loved), and wheezed to her mother that it would fit just fine when she lost fifteen pounds, at which point we all blew Coke out our noses, laughing. Old women, like ourselves, know you should never waste money on so much as a four-dollar tank top that "will fit perfectly when I lose" *any* amount of weight, because we *know* we ain't *ever* gonna lose weight. The universe is expanding and we're all doing our part to help out. The very thought of trying to lose weight to fit into a wedding dress was enough to propel our cola drinks forcefully through our nasal passages and onto the dressing-room mirrors.

The Tammys, by this time, had raided all the bridesmaids dress bins and were merrily slithering into satin and taffeta creations that represented David's vision for the wedding parties of 2002. The question must be asked: Who invented *mauve* and, more important, *why?* It should just be illegal is all—nobody has *ever* looked good in it, and any garment fashioned out of it is rendered irreparably hideous. So, of course, I insisted the Tammys try on *all* the mauve selections.

This is one of the fine points of bridal etiquette. You get to pick your attendants *and* you get to pick what they have to wear. And they have to wear it. And since it is, after all, *your day* and you must be *the* most beautiful one, well, it just doesn't hurt to give yourself every possible advantage by seeing to it that your bridesmaids look like they've been—oh, what's that quaint old saying?—"shot at and missed, shit on and hit." Yes, that's what I had in mind for *my* girls, and didn't they know it.

There was nothing at David's that day quite up to the level of hideous that I had in mind for them, but we did find just the thing for me. It was a big giant long-sleeved, off-the-shoulder, heavily embroidered, pouffy-skirted, bow-butted, train-dragging, blinding-in-its-pure-dee-*whiteness* of a bride's dress that fit me perfectly. Except it was about four to six inches too short, revealing every inch of my white socks and tennis shoes. Perfect. I didn't want to be tripping over my stupid dress when I was trying to dance or stepping on it when I went up stairs. And it was *on sale* for ninety-nine dollars! Clearly, it was Meant to Be. We snapped it up and hauled it outta there. (I'm actually wearing it on the cover of this book—although we rendered it pink for this occasion.) Later, TammyMelanie and TammyCynthia bought those sweet "bride" and "groom" baseball caps for me and the Cutest Boy in the World. I still wear mine all the time.

5

Dressing the Bridesmaids and the Groom

Since we couldn't find any bridesmaids dresses ugly enough to *buy*, we decided to try *renting* them, and all I can tell you is: BING-O! No wonder we couldn't find any hideous dresses to buy— the rental store has been buyin' 'em all up and hoardin' 'em. Oh, yeah, they had some pretty stuff, too, but what fun would *that* be? Since the Queens are of such varying sizes, we couldn't find one style available in sizes to fit all, so we decided to go with a "Southern Belle" theme. The Queens would each rent the most god-awful "Miss Scahhh-litt" dress of her choice. In the process of making their choices, a few minor skirmishes broke out amongst the ranks. For one, TammyDonna discovered that she could also rent a big pouffy petticoat to go under her dress, a revelation she did not share with the others until it was too late for them to also get one. Then Tammy-Melanie got a dress that was the only one with an attached choker necklace above its plunging neckline, and boy, they did *not* like that, which only served to make TammyMelanie love it all the more, and on the night of the wedding, she would reach up, smiling, and fondle it frequently during the course of the evening, which, of course, only further inflamed the choker-less others. New Allison (co-head Wannabe with Our Precious Darlin' George), who came all the way from Afghanistan or Croatia or somewhere far off, where she'd been working that year, showed up with a *hat and a parasol*. I thought then the whole thing was about to degenerate to spittin' and name-callin', but they managed to hold it down to sniffin' and look-ing at her squinty-eyed.

You're no doubt aware of the Sweet Potato Queens' policy stating that one should Never Wear Panties to a Party. If you've ever been married, you also know that too often the "partyin' " slows to a trickle if it don't dry up completely, and this sad state is attributable, by and large, to the insurmountable buttheaded-ness of men. With a nod to this widely accepted fact of marriage, we decided that our undergarments should make a statement. Of course, it made a pretty big statement that we were wearing any a-tall, but that was not enough for us. Why use a feather when the whole chicken is just sitting right there? Indeed. We like to think of ourselves as Whole Chicken girls. So we wore these big giant panties—and when I say "big giant," I need for you to understand that they came to my knees and I'm six-foot-one, so you can only imagine them on the rest of the Queens. Emblazoned on the butt of these big giant panties, in hot pink, were the words GET REAL.

It's no fun wearing entertaining undergarments if nobody *sees* 'em—and that *is* Victoria's secret—so at random intervals throughout the evening, we would, without warning, turn around, bend over, and fling our dresses over our heads, artfully displaying our behinds with their GET REAL legends. Pretty cute and very well received by onlookers. TammyCarol was so taken with this little ritual that she wandered off from the rest of us and was having just the best time performing it for everyone she encountered. The problem was, she did her dress-flinging with her typical boundless joyful enthusiasm, and every time she flung the dress over her head, it would catch in her tiara and one of us would have to unhook her, only to have her repeat the show for another lucky partygoer thirty seconds later.

After a bit, we all tired of chasing her around in order to get her dress off her crown, so we just let her stroll around like that. It was much more efficient, actually: saved her all that bending over and flipping, saved us from the pursuit and unhooking detail, and gave everybody a bird's-eye view of her GET REAL hiney. We shoulda just hooked it up there at the beginning of the night and saved all of us the effort. Live and learn, as usual.

Friends do not make friends wear bows on their butts—words of wisdom from Queen Kathy in South Carolina, who allowed as how her own wedding party photos look like beautiful portraits of the Mormon Tabernacle Choir, since the girls wore navy and the guys wore black. But nobody, not bridesmaids nor groomsmen, were forced to wear bows on their behinds. I *wish* we lived in a time when butt-bows and bustles were required fashion accessories because everybody wanted their butts—if not of homegrown amplitude—to at least *appear* to be as large as possible. I pray to God I live long enough to see and participate in that glorious day.

It's your day and you get to dictate the fashion of every person directly involved. That's a ton of power, little missy—see that you don't abuse it, since Karma makes house calls, I can assure you. These people are your closest friends and relatives—that's why they're being saddled with the great (or perhaps dubious) honor of dancing in attendance at your wedding—so keep that in mind as you start handing down dictums regarding what all you expect of them in this deal.

One bride—who really doesn't need to be named, so many were the dead burned bodies left in her wake—decided she was not going to have any tan lines turning up in *her* wedding photos. Nor any *tans*, either, for that matter. The problem was, the bridesmaids had all giddily planned a beach weekend before the wedding, and when Miss Bride got wind of it, there was a fit pitched that truly qualified as the much-touted "hissy." The bridesmaids gowns were *strapless—hel-lo?* Was she the only one who remembered this salient fact? Big Woe be unto the bridesmaid who showed up at *her* wedding with big ole white tan lines crisscrossing her nekkid shoulders. And since *she* herownself was a true natural-born redheaded person—meaning she was also a true natural-born frog-belly-*white* person—she didn't want there to be too much contrast in the photos between *their* skin and *hers*.

This bride was also concerned that the bridesmaids towered over her, which wasn't hard to do, given that she was about four-foot-nothin', so she insisted that they all wear ballet flats—nothing but the merest hint of a strip of leather between the feet and the floor, nothing to add even a hair to their height. She planned to wear stilettos under her gown to even out the playing field as much as she could. Before it was over, they were all praying she broke at least an ankle, if not her neck, on the way down the aisle.

One note on shoes, however: It prolly is a good idea to have some semblance of a guideline for your attendants' footwear—if you don't, at least one will show up with four-inch platform shoes with clear heels and there will be them big ole ho shoes in the middle of all your photos. Unless, of course, you're *all* planning on wearing ho shoes, in which case blending will be achieved.

Dressing the Bridesmaids and the Groom

Your friends *look* like they *look*. You know what they look like when you ask them to *be* bridesmaids. And although you may foolishly think that you yourself will morph into a different fifty-pounds-lighter, totally-made-over person by the time your big day rolls around—and that's a highly unreasonable demand to make on oneself, even—you simply *cannot* ask and/or expect it from your friends. You cannot say to these women, "I want you to be my bridesmaid because you are one of my nearest and dearest friends, but what I'm reeeally interested in is How We Will All Look in the Photos, so as much as I *do love you* just the way you are, for *this occasion*, it's going to be necessary for you to drop four dress sizes, alter your skin tone and hair color, length, and style, and also pretend to be short."

If your bridesmaids happen to be of diverse sizes, shall we say, meaning that some of them are normal-sized women and some of them are tee-tiny little freaks of nature (like most "normal-sized" and also lazy women, I prefer to think of tee-tiny little people as freaks as opposed to considering the possibility that they are maybe just a tad more willing to eat sensibly and exercise than I am myownself), you should pick out the dress style according to what will look best on the biggest bridesmaid. *Everything* and *anything* will look fine on the tee-tiny little freak women, but a friend with a big ole butt who's forced to march down an aisle wearing a skintight floor-length dress with a fishtail hem will still have her big ole butt when the day is done, but she will no longer be your friend.

I think Queen CeeCee proved herself to be the sweetest and

Queenliest of brides when one of her bridesmaids discovered (after being told that she couldn't have children) that she was *six months* pregnant. CeeCee was so happy for her friend that she told her she would cut the belly out of that bridesmaids dress for her if she couldn't fit in it—or she could wear a T-shirt, maternity shorts, and flip-flops if she wanted to—just as long as she stood up with her at her wedding. Now, that right there is what you call your friend for life.

And for all the hilarious horror stories we hear about errant behavior in the ranks of bridesmaids and groomsmen, occasionally we get glimpses of truly heartwarming acts of loyalty and friendship. For example: Queen Kim was to be a bridesmaid in the wedding of a classmate. She had dutifully performed all her bridesmaidly duties, including attending all functions, making rice bags, buying the awful dress, and having her hair done in an extravagant "up-do" the day of the wedding at the request of the bride, who wanted everybody's hair to "match." As luck (for Kim) would have it, the groomsmen were just *way* cute, and one of them in particular took a very mutual shine to our Queen Kim. Blah, blah, blah, blah . . . Let's cut through all the boring *conversation* and get right to the part where, just a few hours before the wedding, they find themselves together in a Jacuzzi by candlelight, one of them with their head flung back against the side while the other one performed the ancient mating rite of toe-sucking. For the sake of clarity here, it should be noted that Queen Kim's head was the one flung back and the grooms-man was performing the toe-suck on her, not on himself. Okay, so the scene is clear, right? Well, here's something you absolutely need to know and remember at all times, but especially when, for whatever reason, you have your head flung back near lighted candles: Hairspray is *highly* flammable!

Kim was not thinking about this at the time, but if she had been, she likely would not have been so confused by the sudden cessation of the toe-sucking and the odd look of surprise and consternation on the face of the groomsman right before he commenced slapping her upside the head where her extravagant, highly sprayed up-do was burning merrily.

Proving that he was, in fact, a Spud Stud of the highest order, he told her, after the hair-fire was extinguished, "I thought about just dunking you but I didn't want to mess your hair up." Kim merely laughed, shook the ashes out of her bouffant, went to the wedding, had a fabulous time, and apart from an odd smell of singe, nobody detected a thing.

Talk about your rising from the ashes! What a lucky bride to have had such a plucky bridesmaid.

The Groom's Clothes

Okay, I have spoken before, on many occasions, about the inherent dangers of associating oneself with a man of the clotheshorse variety, but just to refresh your memory: If he's spending an excessive amount of time, energy, and money on his own appearance, he will not have enough of any of that to focus on, appreciate, and help to fund *our* appearance, which is way more important. If anybody is gonna be considered to be "arm candy" in this deal, it needs to be *us*.

And while good grooming is a must, trust me, you do not want to marry a man who feels he must shower, shave, and dress snappily just to run out and get you a Sunday paper—it will be Sunday afternoon before he's even ready for the errand, and you will be way crabby by then.

As with so many things in life, there is just a Fine Line to be dealt with here. In my experience, however, the ones who pay too little attention to their own appearance are much easier to deal with (read: fix) than the fancy-pantsers. I personally have never observed any reformation of a dandy—if you've got one, you're stuck with one, and there ain't no modifyin' their behavior. If he's wearing green pants with little blue whales on 'em when you meet him, I pray, for your sake, that you just keep on walkin', 'cause if you don't, I promise you there's a pair of yellow golf knickers in your future.

So we might as well talk about the ones we *can* help (again, read: fix)—the guy whose mama still dresses him, badly; the guy who still dresses like he's in college, in 1975; the guy who buys all his clothes at Wal-Mart, and doesn't even try them on first; and, of course, your regular ole slob.

And here's the only advice I have for you for any of the above: Find the men's store in your town that has the best-looking stuff your guy can afford—and still afford *you*—then hook him up with the best-dressed salesman in there and leave. Do *not* try to dress him yourself—he will end up looking like a girl dressed him, perhaps slightly better than if his mama dressed him but not necessarily, and besides, that's not really the level of improvement we were looking for here.

I remember being on a plane once and a very young couple was seated in the row ahead of me. They couldn't have been married more than a few hours. Her hair was still "done" in the very elaborate up-do that had clearly been created specifically to allow the details on the back of her bridal gown to be shown to best advantage. There were still pearls and other gewgaws scattered about her head. Her professionally applied makeup still radiated. She was dressed casually but smartly, and was a veritable vision of loveliness.

And then there was the groom. He had a bad mullet haircut—and I know you think that's redundant, but believe me, bad as they all are, there really are some gradations (there was some home-barbering involved here, I'm certain). He also had a fairly active case of acne going. (Now, I know that's a terrible affliction and it wasn't his fault, but it *does* tend to have a life expectancy, and I'm of the opinion that we ought not to be marryin' 'em until they are old enough to have outgrown it.) He had on some kind of pooka shell necklace thing with his *tank top*. (Okay, nobody ought ever to have anything to do with any guy who wears a pooka shell necklace—or a tank top, either, for that matter, unless it is, in fact, an athletic event. Let's just say that's a rule from now on—guys in necklaces and/or tank tops or "wife beaters" do *not* get any.) Baggy, butt-showing shorts and flip-flops completed his traveling ensemble.

I looked at her. And I looked at him. After repeating this process several times, it was all I could do to keep from leaning up, tapping her on the shoulder, and just flat-out *asking* her, "Hunny, what *were* you thinking?" But I'm sure it had to have crossed *her* mind by this time, too.

You will need to give him some very strict guidelines for his wedding attire. For example, it doesn't matter what color your bridesmaids dresses are, *nothing* of his—or his groomsmen—should match them. We do not want to see men dressed in tuxedos resembling Easter eggs. Nor do we want to see them in ruffledy shirts in pastel hues. Their stuff should all be pretty much black and white. They should serve as the backdrop for the real show of the day—the bride and her attendants.

Queen CeeCee told me that her very thrifty husband borrowed his father's white patent-leather shoes for their wedding (we did not discuss how or why that father came to be in possession of his own personal pair of white patent-leather shoes—that, clearly, is a discussion for another day). But anyway, the borrowed shoes were too big—so big, in fact, that CeeCee's husband had to stuff the toes of them with newspaper so they would stay on his tiny little feet, which made it so he clomped and looked like he had on clown shoes—big ole *white patent-leather* clown shoes—for the ceremony. But that was not his only cost-saving contribution to the event. He also economized by wearing a pair of white socks he already had, saving the cost of a new pair. This meant that after all the hoopla of the wedding was over and done with, thanks to *him* and *him alone* and his thoughtful and thrifty ways, they emerged from the church not just as husband and wife but also with *money left over.* Of course, it was only enough money to buy a pair of white socks, but *still* . . .

It was not until the wedding photos came back that the truth about those wedding socks was fully revealed, however. The younger readers out there may not remember this, but athletic socks didn't used to be just plain ole white socks. They used to always have some bright color in bands around the tops of 'em. The ones CeeCee's beloved selected for their wedding day—and pictures—had brilliant *red* stripes around the tops, and we know this because they are fully visible, shining clean through the white tux pants, in each and every photograph taken that day.

6

The Greed (Oops, Sorry, the Gifts)

Probably *the* most important task facing you as you plan your wedding is deciding where all you will sign up for presents and what you want on your "must have" list and what will go on your "sure would be nice" supplementary list. You want to make it as easy as possible for everybody who has ever had the slightest contact with you over the course of your entire life to go out and instantly put their hands on the Perfect Gift for you.

Even if your tastes tend to run pretty close to tacky and downright cheesy, you should definitely register for the solid-platinum flat-ware, wineglasses that are hand-blown in a secret grotto by Portuguese fairies, and the actual dinnerware of Empress Josephine. And, of course, you'll include on your list top-of-the-line appliances—anything Viking, naturally—and two-thousand-thread-count sheets. Everyone will be so *impressed* by the über-fine quality of your selections, even if they're confused by the fact that you obviously gave much more thought to your *gift* selection than your *groom* selection. But you can't be concerned about that now—think about it tomorrow. And don't worry that all that stuff will look incongruous in your used double-wide. You can skulk back down there later and exchange it all for melamine and Dixie cups if you want to.

Then there's that other school of thought that concerns itself not one whit with appearances and encourages young brides to reveal all in the pages of their gift registry—right down to pre-ferred sex toys and lube, warming or non. Might as well get what you want to start with is their thinking. I'm thinking it's just a tad too much information for the general public—but that's just me. Queen Deb told me that she personally knows a bride who enclosed a "gift request list" (one item of which was "25-pound bags of kitty litter") with the wedding invitation, and for the guests' utmost convenience, she noted that she and the groom were also listed at, I swear to you, *the Bank of America*. These people are asking for cash and kitty litter? All I can say is either they were raised by wolves or that Bride's mama is dead as a boot 'cause *clearly* they ain't got no *people* to tell 'em how to act.

Down here in Mississippi, one of the main pre-wedding parties held for new brides is called a "Sip and See." This is an occasion when everybody you know—well, every *woman* you know; *straight* men couldn't be dragged to one of these—is invited to come over, drink alcoholic beverages, and goon all the gifts you've amassed so far. There are even people who hire themselves out to come over and artfully arrange all the loot to show it off to the best possible advantage. The gift cards are left attached so that everybody can see not only the gift but who gave it as well. This practice helps foster competition amongst the gift givers, always a good thing for the gift recipient.

I've been to a whole bunch of these in my life, but so far, I ain't seen no sacks of cash and I sure ain't seen no *kitty litter* on the "Sip and See" tables. I don't care *how* many cats you've got, don't be wasting your wedding gifts on kitty litter. Come to think of it, if you've got that many cats, I don't know where you found a husband to begin with, and if he knows about them and is marrying you anyway, he has *got* to be gay.

What We Will Do for Gifts

I don't know about you, but I'm willing to debase myself to just about any degree for some first-class gifts, and let me tell you, a good wedding shower will afford many opportunities for both debasement and first-class gifts. So a shower's a *bonanza*, is all I'm saying. If there's alcohol involved, you can count on a fairly equitable distribution of the debasement, but luckily, all the gifts will go home with *you*.

Thinking up games for women to play at showers—there's a job I wish I had. Of course, the one I really want is the one my friend George says *he* wants. George is a very successful attorney here in Jackson, Mississippi, and he's *tard* (that's "tired," if you're not from around here). To be successful, even *lawyers* have to work hard. This may be news to you, but it's the truth. Nothin's easy—*except* maybe this dream job that George has been talking about: naming paint colors. I gotta tell you, that resonated for me when he said it. What a job! We envisioned just piling up in a big comfy chair in a room with walls of windows, sipping a cup of specially blended coffee, gazing thoughtfully at paint chips, and waiting for the muse to speak to us about the name of the particular color. The colors are all pretty much the same ones you've been looking at since you could focus your eyes; only their *names* have changed. What used to be "beige" became one company's "straw hat" and another one's "linen hanky." Brown is "chocolate chip," which must have been a slow muse day for the Color Namer. I mean, how hard was it to come up with *that*? He worked a little harder on "blue," coming up with "skylark" and "harbor." It drives me nuts when clothing catalogs fall prey to the Color Namer's tricks. If there's a bad print job on the photo of the blue poncho you want to order, "skylark" is no help since a skylark is a *brown* bird. So where does the blue aspect come in? No one knows but the Color Namer, and he ain't talkin'. George agreed with me that, if *we* had that job, the first color we'd officially name would be "Baby Do-Do Green." Is there any *doubt* what color that is?

Paint colors and shower games—who thinks 'em up? Don't know. Shower games just somehow surface at gatherings of women. These activities do not occur among men. Let's see if we can think of a game that a bunch of *men* think up that's comparable to the ones you read about below, and then let's try to picture them doing it. Don't picture it too clearly, however, if you're thinking of marrying one of 'em.

In one game everybody gets a pair of panty hose with a cucumber in one of the feet. Tie the cuke-free leg around your waist, so that your green weenie is swinging free, almost touching the ground. Then everybody gets a softball or a grapefruit. The object is to nudge your ball toward the goal line with your newly acquired appendage. Lots of pelvic thrusting. Timing and rhythm have much to do with who wins. Let's name this one dickball?

A variation on this theme replaces the cucumber with a lemon. Bottles are set up as bowling pins, and the object is to move your hips enough to knock over the pins with your lemon. And this is, what, dick-bowling? Tacky Jackie of Alabama says to tie a smoked *sausage* on a long string and then tie it around your waist and try to ease it in the mouth of a two-liter bottle. She said you could hardly control it at all. Lordamercy, if *that* ain't so! The real ones often can't be controlled, either—by their owners or anybody else. Hunny, I am telling you, a man will go into the pitch-black dark with a hard-on where he wouldn't dare go in the broad daylight with a loaded gun. And that right there is The Truth.

I went to a shower once when, in the middle of our games, a cat commenced caterwaulin' from the next room. The sounds that cat was making were not of this earth, I swear. Everybody just kinda froze as that cat reached—and held—what could only be described as a "fever pitch." We thought surely the cat was being dismembered on the other side of that wall. Eyes were big and round, mouths were gaping in fear and dread. "Oh," said our hostess, in a surprisingly offhand manner, "that's just my Siamese cat, Piwacket. She's in heat." Well. That *did* explain a *lot*—at least to our crowd.

So we tried to go on with the shower games. I think we were playing the one where you have to take a ball of string and pass it through your clothes, up one side and down the other, and into the clothes of the girl next to you, until everybody in the room is completely connected—and snarled—in this big wad of string. (I'm not sure what the point is, but it is a fair analogy for most extended families, is it not?) Anyway, we were trying valiantly to carry on with the frivolity, but the kitty commotion next door was escalating rapidly. To the sounds of her wailing and yowling, she added assorted thumps, bangs, and crashes as she apparently attempted to run *up* the various walls of the room as well as through the solid wood of several doors. Presently, we heard the tearing of fabric as she, in her solitary distress, must have ripped the curtains from the windows. About this time, she uttered the most flesh-creeping shriek of all, at once guttural and shrill. One could not help but grasp its eloquence and sincerity. The silence in our room was broken by someone expressing the sentiment of us all: "We got to find *somebody* to screw that cat." We dissolved in tears of laughter, and as if by magic, the CD changed, and out came the strains of Kacey Jones singing—what else? "We All Need to Get Laid!" Many rousing choruses followed, and we think even the little kitty waxed philosophic about the whole thing. What we needed right then wasn't being offered to the cat or to us. So we did what we've done for time immemorial: We headed for the food!

Yippee! It's Finger~Food Time!

Some of our Very Favorite Food in all the world is Finger Food, which you find in great quantities at your better wedding showers. In fact, the finger food and the punch are the only reasons I can think of right off to *go* to these events, that is, if you are not the gift recipient.

If you've been drinking (and I know you have), you'll want to start off with your salty food group. You need something salty, and it needs to be portable because if there's a big crowd, you may end up sitting on the floor before it's over. (Actually, floor-sitting may have more to do with the happy fact that one cannot fall *off* the floor than with the number of people there.) At any rate, you need some items that can be popped, whole, into one's mouth. Sometimes, through the benefits of alcohol, you'll discover that the capacity of your mouth has been expanded. You should exercise caution during such times. Not only will more fit *into* your mouth, but decidedly, more will come *out* of it—namely words—and they will not fit back in there no matter what.

At one gala event, TammyDonna and I discovered that one particular little niblet—something delectable on a full-sized saltine cracker—was giving other people fits because they were biting it in two and then being covered in cracker crumbs for their trouble. We made the happy discovery that if you just stre-e-e-tched our mouths out sideways—like we were saying "e-e-e-e-e!"—then those whole en-tire crackers would just slide right on in there. We were dazzled by this revelation and, indeed, performed it for each other's enjoyment over and over and over until all the little niblets were safely in our own personal tummies.

Jody's Big Bites

Queen Jody has provided the recipe for those niblets. We call 'em Jody's Big Bites, and they are E-Z. You just mix up **1 tablespoon dillweed, 1 tablespoon caraway seed, 1 tablespoon crushed red pepper, 1 package dry Ranch dressing mix,** and **1½ cups canola oil.** Stir all that up together and divide it between **2 1-gallon Ziploc bags.** Put **2 sleeves of saltines** in each bag and soak 'em overnight. Turn them frequently and make sure they all absorb gobs of the goo. The next morning, pour out any unabsorbed oil and put the crackers in a fresh Ziploc bag. They will stay crispy and be yummy, and if you've had enough to drink, you can fit a whole one in your mouth, easy.

Olive Yum Yums

The other handy finger-food item we have Queen Jody to thank for is the fabulous Olive Yum Yums. These will fit easily into your mouth, no matter what condition you're in. You just soften **4 ounces of cream cheese.** Then drain **a jar of colossal green olives, with pimiento,** naturally. Blot 'em dry, then get a blob of cream cheese and form it into a ball around the olive and then roll the whole thing in **chopped pecans.** You'll need to part with 'em for a little while and let them chill a little bit in the refrigerator to reset the cream cheese. Then you can just eat 'em till you explode!

Mississippi Sin

No wedding shower would be complete without Mississippi Sin—and that's a loaded statement if I ever made one, but I am referring, in this particular case, to *dip* of that name. Now, we most often see this made in a hollowed-out loaf of French bread with the excavated bread hunks used to carry the "sin" to one's mouth. However, you could make it in a *shoe* and eat it off your *toes* and it would be just as good. For the sake of decorum, though, we'll go with the French bread here.

The Greed (Oops, Sorry, the Gifts)

Preheat the oven to 350 degrees. Slice off the top of a **loaf of French bread** and then carve out the middle of it, saving the top for baking. Cut the middle into hunks for dipping later. Mix together **1½ cups sour cream, 2 cups grated sharp Cheddar, 1 8-ounce package cream cheese, ⅓ cup chopped green chiles, and ⅓ cup chopped green onions.** Stuff all that into the bread shell. Put the top back on and wrap up the whole thing in heavy foil. Bake it for an hour. Dip away. It's good on *anything*, and the "sin" is how dang good it is.

7

Vows, Prenups, and Kiss~Offs

Okay, here's an important feature of a wedding you need to keep foremost in your mind whenever you think of your beloved and start practicing writing your "new name" all over stuff and your eyes glaze over and you're thinking how you could just sop him up with a biscuit. (In the South, anything worth eating is likely to be liberally covered in a delicious gravy; to "sop" is to avail oneself of every particle of tongue-tingling bliss by dragging one's biscuit, also a staple of fine Southern dining, over every inch of one's plate, rendering the plate spotless and leaving one's taste buds and tummy totally tickled.) Just remember, that wedding you've dreamed of and planned and sweated over will result in your being a fractional partner in a *marriage*. How big your part of the fraction will be remains to be seen and, indeed, may vary over time. Marriage is a legally binding (as in hand-cuffing, hog-tying, ham-stringing, and otherwise trussing up) *contract*. What that means, for starters, is that no matter what, *this* is the guy you'll watch walking *your own daughter* down the aisle at her own wedding one day, years hence, God willing. After you sign that paper, there is just no getting rid of him completely *ever*, no matter what, short of his own untimely death, which hardly *ever* happens when you want it to, so don't count on it, and we are completely *against* the actual killing of 'em yourownself. As gratifying as it might momentarily be, you *will* regret it when the law comes calling.

What you need is a good prenup to make sure you're safe. Our top legal adviser, banana pudding maker, and Official Ass-Coverer, TammyCynthia, wrote up a splendid and very livable prenup for TammyMelanie, who recently found herself marrying the love of her life, Sugar Bear. (I will explain in a little while how TammyMelanie "found herself marrying" him; it's the Best Wedding Story ever in the history of the entire world, living or dead.) I offer below the TammyCynthia Prenup, free but for the price of this book, and you should feel free to use it in defense and preservation of your own life. (It would be the Nice Thing to Do if you were to send TammyCynthia a Free-Will Love Offering of not less than $34 and not more than $9,999—or whatever you think her Saving Your Ass will be worth to you in the years to come. Let your conscience be your guide, as they say. It would mean so much to her and help her get that operation so she could run and play like the other lawyers.)

THE TAMMYCYNTHIA PRENUPTIAL CONTRACT

THE STATE OF _____
COUNTY OF _____
These vows are to be made on this the ____ day of _____, 20__, between the interested parties, _____ (hereinafter "Wife") of _____ County, _____ (state), and _____(hereinafter "Husband") of _____ County, _____ (state).

WHEREAS, both parties are above the age of 18 years and notwithstanding sage counsel of their peers, i.e., TammyCynthia (hereinafter "Rocket Scientist") Speetjens, wish to become Husband and Wife.

WHEREAS, both parties enter into this relationship fully cognizant of their respective rights and obligations, or at least as cognizant of anything as either of them has ever been, which clearly isn't much, and,

WHEREAS, both parties wish to establish an efficient mechanism for resolving the innumerable differences which they anticipate will arise throughout their married lives, and,

WHEREAS, the parties desire to set forth their agreements and understandings herein;

NOW, THEREFORE, in consideration of the foregoing, of the mutual promises herein set forth, of the invaluable loss of personal freedom and dignity, and of other good and sufficient considerations, the receipt of which is hereby acknowledged, the parties agree as follows:

1. *Purposes. The purposes of this marriage are manifold: to provide companionship during two clearly undirected and juvenile lives; to pool economic resources in order to forestall either one of them from completely ruining the other; to provide a convenient source of blame for whatever occurs (particularly to Wife) short of nuclear attack, either together or individually; and to vent either party's wanton, shameful, animalistic, and choreographically silly physical desires.*

2. *Term. The marriage shall be solemnified on or about _____ and will last a lifetime regardless of HOW CUTE anybody is who comes over when one party may happen to be out of town, regardless of HOW LONG that party may have been out of town.*

3. *Expenses. Husband and Wife agree to share equally the expenses of maintaining the household. Additionally, Husband agrees to limit his monthly expenditures for ties or other Beau*

Brummel–like items to One Hundred Dollars, which amount may be increased only upon the written agreement of both parties. Any amount not spent in a given month shall lapse. Wife may spend as she pleases without regard to any condition, including, but not limited to, Husband's ability to obtain food.

4. *Decisions. The parties recognize that numerous decisions must be made each day that affect the parties together or individually, and recognize, too, the necessity for a decision maker in the event of their inability to agree on a proper solution to any particular problem. In consideration of Wife's gender-related superior intellect, Wife shall be the final arbiter on any such differences.*

5. *Marital Relations. The parties agree to have a lot of those.*

6. *Personal Habits. The parties hereto covenant and agree that neither will smoke cigarettes nor wear anything that looks particularly goofy, except at events of extreme spiritual and moral significance, such as their wedding.*

7. *Warranties. Wife herein warrants that she cannot, nor will not, attempt to cook under any circumstances. Husband warrants that he will eat whatever is put in front of him, regardless of from whence it came, and will be damn glad to get it.*

8. *Default. In the event of a breach by either party of any condition or warranty herein which binds such party, the defaulting*

*party may utilize any of the following remedies: (1) free week-
end at resort of choice, (2) unlimited massage therapy, (3) free
liquor forever.*

Vows

Now that the prenup is out of the way, we need to address the
actual nupping. What is it we're willing to get in front of a
whole bunch of witnesses and swear we'll do for the *rest* of our
lives? I can tell you, this is one of your very short lists. You'll
definitely be willing and highly motivated to breathe in and
breathe out all day, every day, no matter what, but beyond
that, you're gonna find that your likes and dislikes, your want-
to's and your don't-want-to's, will fluctuate a lot. While we
want *them* to be swearing on a stack of Bibles that they will
tote us around on a little pillow for the rest of our natural lives
and all that that entails, we want to leave ourselves some
breathing, if not actual wiggle, room. You yourself, the wife-to-
be, should write the vows. Don't rely on some old standard
written eons ago with the obvious goal of improving the quality of life for *men*. The groom's vows should be lengthy and
detailed and all-inclusive with regard to the worship, adoration,
and care of you.

Regarding anything vowlike from you, the bride, he should
consider himself a blessed man that you're willing to marry up
with him at all and to stand up in front of God and everybody

and promise to try real hard not to murder him in his sleep in the years to come. For example, you cannot say for sure that you will love and adore forever and ever the *china pattern* you picked out, yet you *can* say with absolute certainty that those dishes are not ever going to do anything that will hurt, shame, irritate, or enrage you. You can't promise to cherish them always, but you could probably issue a limited warranty that you won't smash them all to bits one day—on purpose, anyway. Accidents *do* happen, as we all know, and that's regrettable, but too often they're simply unavoidable.

If the preacher tries to trick you into promising a bunch of unrealistic stuff, you should just vague him off with a giggle and a non-answer. (My friend Colleen said her grandmother used a similar technique when she found herself confronted by a new mother bearing a homely baby and expecting a complimentary reaction. Granny would clap her hands and say with great enthusiasm, "My-y-y-y! What a baby!") Just remember, your cousin's idiot husband is no doubt videotaping your wedding from the balcony, so there *will* be a court-admissible record of what all you actually do promise to do here, so choose your words with the utmost care.

This is where the choice of ministers can be an important factor. He or she should definitely be a friend of the bride and willing to help you commit to as little as possible while extracting blood oaths from your beloved. If you can't find a clergy person willing to assist you in this regard, at least choose one whose personal foibles will distract the audience long enough for you to skate by the vowing stuff. For instance, the minister at one Queen's wedding was tongue-tied, and his continued repetition of the word *marriage*, or in his case, "mawwaige," kept the entire wedding party and congregation teetering on the brink of erupting into unanimous guffaws throughout the ceremony.

Queen DareDevil Dahlin's preacher kinda got carried away with the little sermonette she agreed to let him give during the service. The preacher started rambling on about men in general, apparently forgot where he was, and went off into "Men are just funny sometimes. We like to hold everything inside when we're mad and, y'know, that's not good for us, so we just head down to the titty parlor and blow off some steam." Now, Queen D thought she was hallucinating and she leaned over to Bert-the-Groom and whispered, "Did he just say 'titty parlor'?" and Bert-the-Groom whispered back, "Yes. He did." And they started snorting and giggling, and the whole church started snorting and giggling. The preacher realized he'd wandered off into some area normally known as "personal problem," and he wrapped it all up pretty quickly after that. So Queen D didn't have to say too much a-tall.

It helps if you've got yourself a groom who's willing to venture into previously uncharted territory, behavior-wise. The day before Queen Teri's brother Mike's wedding, he was semi-whining about how the bride gets her own special entrance song—the whole "Here Comes the Bride" thing—and how it just seemed danged unfair to him that the groom was not afforded a similar consideration. The fact that no one *should* have been surprised at what he pulled at the wedding did not prevent them from *being* surprised, although *dumbstruck* is probably a better description for it. The best man entered the sanctuary and then, suddenly, the lights dimmed and the unmistakable opening strains of *2001: A Space Odyssey* boomed through the air as Mike-the-Groom came out doing Elvis karate kicks and arm-flails. The preacher nearly had to leave the room. This lucky bride was bulletproof is all I'm saying.

One final note: I advise you to make sure that whoever walks you down that aisle is totally on your side, no matter what. This person—whether it's your dad, some other relative, or your best girlfriend—should ask you, as Queen Misty's dad did right before you get to the actual altar, "You sure about this? 'Cause there's an exit right over there, and we can make a break for it if you wanna." And he should be sure he's actually willing to flee with you, should you answer in the affirmative.

Check Your Temp

Okay, you've found the guy, gotten the ring, and made all manner of people—relatives, close and distant, as well as a mess of folks lucky enough to *not* share DNA with you—jump through innumerable hoops in the Planning of Your Special Day. Ridiculous, otherwise unusable, garments have been purchased or rented by assorted persons who can ill afford them—yourself included. Flowers, food, and photographers have been ordered; invitations bought, paid for, addressed, mailed, received, and

RSVP'd to. The world has revolved around you and this blasted wedding for the last 365 days. It's finally time for the culmination of it all—and your feet are feeling just the *slightest* bit chilly.

You're having Second Thoughts—and maybe some third and fourth ones as well. I say that is a very good thing. You need to be thinking *seriously* about what you're fixing to do here, little missy. Granted, a more *opportune* time to do all this second-third-, and fourth-level thinking would admittedly have been 365 days ago, but it is *still* not too late. Just because all of these people have done and spent all that they have done and spent on your behalf and at your request does *not mean* that you have to go through with it. No, ma'am, you most decidedly do not.

But you *have* got to step up to the plate and look 'em all in the eye, every single solitary one of them, starting with the *groom* and moving down through the ranks of parents, wedding party, and various service providers, and just 'fess up and tell 'em *all* that you are inexplicably and possibly permanently Out of the Mood and this wedding will not be happening after all.

And then you've got to stand there and take whatever they dish out. You don't have to let them talk you back into the wedding—and you probably shouldn't—but they are all entitled to bitch you out to any extent they feel so moved, and you are required to listen and nod with empathy and understanding. Well, okay, so you don't have to *actually* listen—you can completely zone out and carry on in your mind with whatever you thought of that's *better* than going through with this wedding—but you must appear to listen, and you must nod with what *appears* to be empathy and understanding, on account of all these people have expended great amounts of time, energy, effort, and actual U.S. dollars on your wimpy ass and they deserve *some* satisfaction—even if all they can get is the pleasure of hollering at you.

You cannot under *any* circumstances just *run off* and leave everybody who cares about you to believe that you have been abducted and/or murdered by strangers and/or aliens, which will bring about the launch of nationwide searches involving overwhelming and exhausting man-hours for law-enforcement personnel and representatives of the media, prayer vigils in countless churches, the costly and humiliating administration of lie-detector tests to persons *formerly* close to you, and the tearful on-air pleadings of your very own mama and daddy for your safe return when in *truth* you have purchased a freakin' bus ticket *the week before* and run off to Las Vegas like the inconsiderate ass-monkey you are.

And if you *still* insist on doing this after much thought and my own personal warnings to the contrary, then at some point early in this charade, you must summon anything resembling balls in your spineless character and pick up a phone and tell somebody The Truth and then take your lumps as described. You must not, under *any* circumstances, pick up a pay phone and call the damn FBI and *lie* to *them* with some mealy-mouthed bullshit about being kidnapped and *raped*, for God's sake. There are *waaaay* too many women being kidnapped and raped every single day for your sorry ass to be using that as a *ruse* to worm your way out of the mess that was entirely, beginning to end, constructed by *you*. And if you do this, I hope they put your sorry ass in jail and give you some time to think about just eggzackly *how* selfish you really are. At the very least, you should have to do the same number of community-service hours that all those cops put in looking for your sorry ass, and pay back all the money your family and friends spent on that silly wedding that wasn't.

I mean, nobody held a gun to your head and demanded that you have a huge, elaborate, ridiculously expensive wedding—or even a small, discreet one. *Unless*, of course, you happen to *be* Ana Maria Cioaba, princess daughter of the self-proclaimed King of the Gypsies in Romania, who at the ripe old age of twelve was dragged, literally, kicking and screaming, to a church and forced to marry a fifteen-year-old groom named Birita. Ana Maria and her bridesmaids, who were very supportive of her resistance, briefly took shelter in a nearby house and refused to come out, shouting, according to news reports, "slogans against the groom."

After a bit, the reluctant bride did emerge and slogged over to the church, where her father performed the ceremony himself, after which she stalked out and refused to look at the groom snuffling along behind her. The father's "adviser" had announced that the wedding would take place, with her or without her (not sure how *that* works), and either way, she'd be beaten for disrupting the lavish event. They were all pissed that the suckling pig got cold, I guess.

Okay, if you are *twelve* and somebody is actually holding a gun to your head or threatening in a convincing manner to beat you about the head and body unless you marry somebody of *any* age, then, and only then, do you have permission—even *encouragement*—to run like mad, and tell any lie you have to to anybody you have to tell it to to get the hell away. And call us. We'll come help you any way we can—including, but not limited to, shouting slogans against the groom and his mommern 'em.

If you *do* decide to skip your wedding, here's something to consider: The Loews hotel in New Orleans offers a Runaway Bride package deal. For a mere $485 a night, you get a private palm reader to predict your uncertain future, diamond resetting recommendations from the concierge, a look-changing haircut (color will cost extra, I imagine, but you'd expect that), your calls screened, and an in-room viewing of Julia in *Runaway Bride*.

And as long as you're in N.O. celebrating, you should know that there's simply *no* better place for carryin' on in the wee-wee hours than at the the F&M Patio Bar on Tchoupitoulas Street, owned by my nephew, Trevor Palmer. Consistently voted *the* best late-night bar, with the best bar food and the best juke-box, Trevor's place has even got a leopard-skin-covered pool table that doubles as a "dance floor" for particularly exuberant celebrants. (The F&M Patio had previously belonged to my seester Judy's ex-husband. You'll have to read *her* book, *Southern-Fried Divorce*, to find out how it came to be Trevor's.)

8

Things to Avoid, if Possible, on Your Wedding Day

If you've been living with the groom for the last five years and the two of you have three children ranging in age from seven years to six months and you're visibly pregnant *again*, unless you just have a really wicked sense of humor, not to mention irony, you might *not* want to choose "We've Only Just Begun" as your wedding anthem.

Even if the wedding is outdoors, it's generally considered impolite for any of your bridesmaids or groomsmen to smoke during the ceremony. If this is a potentiality within your *inner circle*, there's not much hope for curbing the behavior of your common garden-variety *guest*, and I think you should probably prepare yourself that there may be spitters amongst them as well. If the groom is someone called Charlie the Stump, you probably could have foreseen this eventuality long before even the second date, and it now falls under the "made bed, must lie in it" category. Oh, well.

Have someone frisk all members of the wedding party for hidden flasks. Even if it is a very long service, it is not ever acceptable for any person standing at the front of the gathering to whip out even the most cleverly disguised vessel and furtively sip from it—mainly because then everybody *else* will want some and it deteriorates into elbow-nudging and whispering and whining and passing and grabbing and more, and then louder whispering about who is getting more than their share. There are several ways to avoid this, and the best is to have a very short service to insure that even your thirstiest attendees can make it through without a pit stop. If you insist on dragging the thing out, then you might want to just have the ushers hand everybody a small flask with their program so they can numb themselves at will during the service.

Queen Fifi advised against having a handsome six-foot-four meat carver at the reception, if one's mother is a tad on the trashy side. Apparently, Feef was on the guest list at a soiree once where this happened and the mother of the bride absconded with the meat carver, and the disgruntled dad was left to carve the meat his ownself. The meat, reportedly, was hacked viciously and slapped onto the plates of confused and wary partygoers. Not festive.

A nameless Queen, who knows who she is, cautions us against serving M&M's in little paper cups at outdoor weddings. A little-known fact is that squirrels *love* M&M's and will brave just about anything to get at them. Another little-known fact: While M&M's may not melt in your hand, they *will*, however, melt if a squirrel steps on 'em on a hot day—resulting in little brightly colored squirrel tracks on the tablecloths.

Unless you've had extensive training at one of those Southern Belle historical reenactment events at an antebellum mansion in Natchez, Mississippi, you probably want to avoid wearing a hoop skirt. If you insist on wearing one, though, this would *not* be a good time to adhere to our "Never Wear Panties to a Party" rule. That thing *will* be up over your head at least once before the party's over.

Queen Laurie advises us to make sure the church doesn't have any "improvement" projects in the works for the week of your wedding. Say, for instance, they plan to refinish the pews that week, as they did for Laurie's wedding. You'll want to make sure they have several days to *dry* before you set your guests' behinds on 'em lest they arise to leave with wood stains on their butts.

Some Canadian Queens wrote to tell me that, since gay marriages were legalized in Ontario, there were a few new rules to consider. For instance, you may not know it's bad luck if either of the grooms has dated the preacher.

A green-tree car freshener with a photo of the bride and groom stapled to it is *not* a suitable party favor.

If you're currently vying for the Wedding Party of the Year slot in your local newspaper or glossy magazine, consider the following for the "Definite Don'ts" department: You know those big giant champagne glasses you see everywhere now that are for, like, *decoration*, never intended to be actual drinking vessels for humans? Well, Queen Karen from Milwaukee told me she was at an announcement soiree, where both the prospective bride and her intended groom had one (the things held an en-tire bottle of champagne apiece), and they decided that whichever one of 'em finished their glass first would be the reigning King or Queen of their future new household. There were apparently no penalties for falling down, picking fights, or puking. What a lovely way to launch your nuptials. And *such* memorable pictures for your wedding album.

The groom should counsel his groomsmen against making references to the breasts of any females, whether they're in attendance or not. My friend Sam Prestridge swears to me that he actually witnessed a groomsman meeting the mother of the bride for the first time, and by way of greeting, he seized the woman's hands and, stretching her arms out wide, joyfully exclaimed, "OOOOOOO-WEEEEE! *Now* I know where Sally [the hapless bride] got all them titties!" If you mention this to your intended groom and he doesn't understand why this would necessarily be a bad precaution, reconsider your choice of grooms.

If anybody is just really dead-set against this marriage, do everything humanly possible to ensure that that person (or persons) does not attend the wedding. If it's like, the groom's *mother,* in other words someone you really and truly cannot just *not* invite, then by all means create one special invitation—just for her—with the wrong date, time, and location on it. My friend Lynn's high school chemistry lab partner had been in love with her boyfriend for three years. He had already graduated and was in premed, and the two of them planned to marry in June, right after Lynn's friend graduated from high school. No, she was not pregnant. But the mother of the groom was bound and determined to throw herself in the path of true love and "save her son." The woman called or visited in person every friend and relative on both sides of the deal, begging for help in putting a stop to all this. "This girl is going to ruin his life, blah blah blah."

At the wedding, which did take place despite her very intense machinations, the mother of the groom slowly trudged down the aisle, heavily draped in black from head to toe, including a very large black hat with a very long, very dense veil. She looked like something out of an old Bette Davis movie. Everybody pretended not to notice. The mother of the bride came in looking very mother of the bridey and happy. If her tolerance and gracious nature were feeling the strain, it was not readily apparent to the enthralled guests.

Once the ceremony began, the mother of the groom let out a wail that would have drawn prompt law-enforcement response had she done so in the streets. Truly yowling, she was. When the minister tried to gloss over the "any objections" part, rightly fearing the worst, she stood up and yelled, "She's ruining his life! She's ruining his life! Oh! My poor son! How can she do this to him?!" She carried on in this manner all the way through the service, and at the end she flung herself to the floor, sobbing, "His life is over. She's ruined his life."

The wedding party filed out of the sanctuary, the groom grinning in true new-groom fashion, the bride gritting her teeth, the bride's parents absolutely stone-faced, and everybody else in the room swallowing their handkerchiefs in a superhuman effort not to laugh.

Cut to the receiving line at the reception. The mother of the newly minted groom stood there with everybody else and shook hands with the guests, all of whom did their dead-level best to act like she was a normal human being. As they offered their congratulations, instead of the usual "Thank you so much. How wonderful to have you here on this special day!" the groom's mother murmured to each of them, "Well, you *know* she has just ruined his life. I had such high hopes for that boy, and now it's all just a disaster," never missing a beat. (You just ought to live Down Here. You don't know what you're missing.)

Epilogue: Groom graduated from one of the best medical schools in the country and is a highly respected physician. Woman Who Ruined His Life worked as a lab tech while he was in school and now runs a diagnostic lab. They are still married, and by the time you read this they will have celebrated their thirty-ninth wedding anniversary! No word on how they've celebrated the last forty Mother's Days.

9

Wedding Receptions

Queen Roxanne from central Pennsylvania says that, for some inexplicable reason, most wedding receptions in her hometown are held in fire halls. She had no idea how or why this got started, and I was of no help whatsoever in unraveling what clearly *is* a mystery. I mean, even if, once upon a time, the fire hall was the only building available for public gatherings, don'tcha reckon they've erected at least a few more buildings in the ensuing years? You've got to wonder what the attraction is. Now, don't get me wrong, I love me a good fireman as much as the next girl, but I'm still not seeing the universal appeal of having one's wedding reception at the fire station.

Then I heard from a precious—and precocious—fourteen-year-old girl, Elizabeth Joanne, who, having read my books, considered herself sooo lucky to have the Queens as role models; we, of course, agree. Her suggestion for guaranteed wedding reception hilarity was flaming hookers. She hastened to explain herself: She was not endorsing the immolation of women of ill repute as a means of entertaining one's guests, but rather the quaint custom of setting fire to small glasses of alcoholic beverages before quaffing them. This practice is apparently de rigueur at weddings in her own family. Having witnessed it many times in her tender years, she cautioned us that if we opted to try it for our ownselves, we should drink *fast* before the thing gets too hot.

Now, little Elizabeth Joanne did not indicate her geographic area of residence, but it's just possible that she lives somewhere in central Pennsylvania, I suppose—and that *could* account for the popularity of fire halls for wedding receptions, as you would want to be able to offer your guests the comfort and laudable benefit of prompt extinguishment should they inadvertently set themselves on fire during a particularly long-winded toast.

Alcohol is a force to be reckoned with at any gathering, but particularly at weddings. Individuals closely involved with the ceremony in varying capacities may find themselves exceptionally nervous prior to the occasion, and this could lead to gross errors in judgment as to one's personal capacity for the efficient and mannerly processing of alcoholic beverages. People may get drunk at your wedding and fuck it up, and one of those people may be you.

Picture it: The best man (drunk) gets up to make his toast and expounds eloquently enough except for one teeny, tiny, little, hardly even noticeable mistake—he uses the name of the groom's *first* wife. And the groom (drunk) *laughs.* Loud. The bride (drunk) gives everybody a big ole white-gloved finger, then flounces out of the room and stays gone for over an hour, leaving her guests with nothing to do but, you guessed it, get *more* drunk.

You get to choose the groom, but unfortunately, *he* gets to choose the groom*men*, and that can spell d-a-n-g-e-r for you and your perfect wedding day. We all hear tales all the time about the groom's *men* getting the groom blind drunk and thinking it is the height of hilarity to put him on a plane to Alaska without telling anybody. Any enterprise that involves having to fool with drunk guys is pretty much on a collision course with disaster. That anybody ever manages to put on a wedding under these circumstances (meaning having guys in it) is nothing short of miraculous. But even if they don't manage to abscond with the groom, don't be heaving *too* big a sigh of relief—there's plenty more for 'em to fuck up.

Now, the guy we just talked about *accidentally* (we're giving him a large dose of doubt-benefit here) called the new bride by the old bride's name. But Queen Susan had committed on her, a deliberate act of malice, with actual aforethought and exchange of currency. She'd been busier than a one-armed monkey with six dicks planning the Perfect Wedding to this big-shot attorney. (Now, that right there was a mistake she clearly sees in hindsight. Don't *ever* marry a big-shot attorney on account of if you need to divorce him one day, you'll play hell getting anybody to represent you. Well, our Susan has learned *that* part and we appreciate her sharing that little tip with us all.) Anyway, she had every single solitary detail of the wedding worked out, down to the timing of every single song the deejay would play to achieve the maximum effect. Imagine her surprise, then, when the very first song Ratbastard DJ (as she calls him) blasted over the big giant speakers *she* was paying for was George Jones singing "He Stopped Loving Her Today." Susan has in her wedding album photos of herself with her wedding dress hiked up, running flat-footed across the lawn in a wild fury to address the matter with the Ratbastard. The deejay cowered and confessed that one of the groomsmen had given him a hundred bucks to play it—*as a joke*. Well, just ha-fucking-ha! is all I can say.

It's a good idea to have a preview of just what the best man plans to say in his "toast" to the bride and groom at the reception, Queen HunnyBunny points out. The one delivered at her wedding went something like this: "To love, to marriage, to all the kisses we've snatched—and vice versa." Much champagne was spewed from many noses.

My friend Cheryl said she and her then-husband once had a multi-wedding day—as guests, not participants—and this meant multiple champagne opportunities for said *ex*. So much so that by the last reception of the evening, he slipped the bride his *tongue* in the reception line. Another "among the injured" write-ups was inevitable—as was Cheryl's divorce.

One sweet bride told me that at her wedding "everything was fine until the boys started doing shots," and isn't *that* just one of your global truths? Her new hubby came over to dance with her and proceeded to spin her around and around in circles until they both got sick. An inexplicably *sober* groomsman had to drive them to their hotel, where he deposited them at the front door and fled the premises. Bridey managed to get them checked in at the desk, and there being no bellman on duty at that hour, she draped her darling new husband over her *back*, hauled him to the room, and dragged his drunk ass over the threshold. I'm sure that was just the way she'd imagined it since she was a wee tyke playing dress-up.

Now, that does raise a question. When we were growing up and being spoon-fed romantic tales of brides and grooms and weddings and vine-covered cottages with white picket fences, how come nobody *ever* chimed in with any *hints* about how we might have to forgo being the one carried over the threshold? You *know* this wasn't the first time this kind of thing happened. How come nobody ever blabs about it when it might actually do some good? Well, I'm doing my part. It's up to y'all to pay attention and take heed.

My friend Chris—whose covert-operations name is Duchess Wombat—says to make damn sure you know what will be going on simultaneously in other parts of the building where your reception is being held. Chris was chagrinned and not at all pleased to discover, upon her arrival at her own personal wedding reception, that being held in the very next *room* there was a banquet for the contestants in the *Miss Illinois Pageant*. That's right, on her *wedding day*, the one day of her *en*-tire life when *she* is supposed to be the center of the universe's attention and the undisputed *most* beautiful one for miles around, Chris finds herself one door down from a pack of eighteen- to twenty-four-year-old beauty pageant contestants—oh, excuse me, *scholarship seekers*. Suffice it to say, none of the *bridesmaids* got her fair share of attention that night either, so *they* were pretty disgruntled, too. The groomsmen—dogs in tuxes, all— did an inordinate amount of hall-sauntering, and one by one, they fell prey to scholarly discussions with the girls next door.

And on an entirely other note, I'd really like to discourage you from using your wedding reception as your own personal fund-raising event. Yes, I'm talking about the Dollar Dance. This is where you, the bride, in all your radiant splendor, rise and all the men at the party stand in line and wait for their "opportunity" to dance with you, and for this "opportunity," they must pay you, the bride, a *dollar*. Meanwhile, on the other side of the dance floor, your *groom* has his own line of dollar-wielding female guests. Why don't y'all just install a coupla poles and do some real bumpin' and grindin' for your guests, flinging your wedding garments at them until they are in a white-hot frenzy for the two of you? Then they can plaster your sweaty bodies with some real cash. I mean, if you want to make some money on this deal, I'm thinking you need to give 'em a little more for their investment.

Queen Marty told me that she once got a wedding invite that said, "We would like to request your *presents* at our weddin'." Naturally, she attended just to see what all went on and she was not disappointed. Tacked to the wall of the *fire hall* where the reception was held were hundreds of balloons—in the bride's colors, of course—and guests were invited to *purchase* these lovely "decorations." After the balloons were duly paid for—cash only, I'd imagine—the guests were instructed to pop the balloons, surely quite a concert. Then, once the balloons were popped, the guests were further invited to perform the task written on the little slips of bride-colored paper inside. For example: "Kiss the bride and give her five dollars." Talk about your Ponzi scheme! These people have already *paid* for the fucking balloons, and now they're being asked to fork over *more* cash? I bet they'd be willing to pay some *serious* money to *leave* with the assurance that they'd be removed from the family's future "guest" lists.

Food

Whenever anybody's telling me about a wedding they've attended, I want to know what all they had to *eat*. In fact, I want *detailed* descriptions of both clothing and food. As I said earlier, my sister, Judy, shares this affinity. We're shallow and don't mind saying so. We seek only to be entertained—never informed. We know too much stuff already, and some of it is danged hard to forget. Anyway, bad eats are entertaining only if we're sneering at an event to which we were not invited. If we're in attendance, we want reeeally *good* eats and plenty of 'em. Not being big drinkers, we don't care if there's any booze or not, particularly, but then the bar *does* keep the drinkers away from the food, which is *our* domain. And of course, it's *always* entertaining to observe and later dissect the behavior of any guests who might have been "overserved."

At a stand-up affair, like a typical wedding reception, it's important that the finger food actually *be* food that can easily be eaten with the fingers—and preferably in one bite. No fair serving hunks of meat products that are too large to fit easily and completely inside one's mouth. Which is worst, trying unsuccessfully to bite a hunk of pork tenderloin in two and ending up either (a) wrenching it around so that you can gnaw it with your sharper eyeteeth, (b) yanking on it and tearing it with your front teeth, or (c) cramming the whole thing in your mouth and then trying to chew with some discretion and zero drooling? You'll be a vision, no matter what.

And don't you hate it when the bread on the finger sammiches is really fresh and it makes a big glob of immovable dough on the roof of your mouth, not to mention your front teeth? Tasty as it may be, it does create a ticklish etiquette dilemma for one. Hard to carry on polite, benign conversation with one's fellow guests while desperately needing one's tongue to unobtrusively dislodge the glob. There's just no mannerly method of sucking wet bread off one's front teeth in public. That's why, as a guest, you should fill your purse and/or pockets with as many finger sammiches as possible to eat later in bed by yourself. And mercy, if you're the actual *bride* at this affair, you do *not* want a bunch of pictures depicting *you*, in your full bridal regalia, sucking feverishly on your own teeth (or anybody else's for that matter). It does not look virginal at all.

One exception to the "one bite" rule, I think, would be the Krystal hamburger. I have noted, with no small degree of dee-light, a recent development in the advertising and wedding bid-nesses where everybody involved conspires with a local radio station to have a big contest, and the winner gets her wedding "done" by the radio station and its participating sponsors. One lucky bride in Atlanta (actually, in the suburb of Marietta, pro-nounced by the residents as "May-retta") won a wedding recep-tion catered by the local Krystal hamburger establishment. If you don't have Krystals where you live, it's a mystery to me why you still live there. They are little square "burger tiles" smoth-ered in onions and encased in very soft, steamy buns. Perfect is what they are. I personally, being older than dirt, can remember when they were a dime apiece—ten cents a burger!—and so were the fries. And they were open twenty-four hours! So if one found oneself to be a mite peckish and pretty much broke at the end of an evening of carousing, one could root through the nether reaches of one's purse and happen upon a stray *quarter*, and it was *bonanza* time. I liken that feeling of utter elation to what Thomas Edison must've felt when the lightbulb finally came on. Even though I know it's pretty much worthless now, whenever I'm rooting around in the farthest reaches of my purse and my fingers detect the familiar shape and size of that stray twenty-five-cent piece, I still get a fleeting feeling that I've won the lottery.

Krystal hamburgers, should you elect to serve them to your lucky reception guests, would be an exception to the stipulation that food reception must be finger-worthy and one-bite-sized, because Krystals are so very easily bitten into manageable mouthfuls. Oh sure, you might encounter the occasional stubborn pickle slice, but I find that no matter how much you've got crammed into your mouth at one time, there's pretty much always room for a pickle slice.

Now, me, I'm pretty demanding when it comes to cake at a wedding. I mean, it's usually a big giant cake, which, in itself, is pretty exciting, believing as I do that *more is more*, so if it turns out to be gaggy, then it is just soooo depressing. But, first and foremost, in my opinion, it has at least got to *be* a cake. I am not interested in a big pile of Ding Dongs subbing for a groom's cake, and as much as I do dearly *love* Krispy Kremes, they will not come close to appeasing my desire for actual wedding *cake*.

Whatever kind it is, the wedding cake needs to absolutely *reek* of butter. Few things in this world smell anywhere near as good as a big ole snootful of buttercream frosting. You could *almost* be just as happy smelling it as eating it—with the emphasis on "almost." (I read one of those ubiquitous diet-tip columns suggested that instead of *eating* those fattening foods we crave so much, we merely *sniff* them. *Clearly* written by a practicing and devoted anorexic, no?) Make it as plain or fancy as your heart desires—just make sure it tastes divine. And make sure I get a big piece with lots of icing.

And let's just talk for a minute here about this cake-decorating bidness. Queen Debi, a Barn Queen from North Carolina, went to a wedding where there was a real live working fountain smack in the middle of the wedding cake. It had columns running through the middle of the cake that the water went through and moatlike basins on several levels that the water cascaded into, and a winding staircase with little plastic bridesmaids and groomsmen leading up to the tip-top platform, which held the little plastic bride and groom.

And the bride's *color*—she only had *one* and it was a doozy—*lavender,* and so all of the bridesmaids (flesh and plastic) were dressed, head to toe, in all things lavender. They carried lavender-colored bouquets (the flowers did not naturally occur in this shade; they had been dyed to match), and the groomsmen (likewise, real and artificial) wore lavender ruffledy shirts with lavender boutonnieres. Every flower and candle in the church and on the tables in the reception hall was lavender. An *archway* through which all guests passed to enter the reception hall was made of lavender artificial flowers and lavender balloons. The plates, napkins, plastic forks, and glasses? Lavender. Flowers on the cake? Lavender. Rice bags? Ditto. The actual *rice?* But of *course.* Even the very *water* flowing through the in-cake fountain was lavender.

Don't do this.

But if you *do*, oh, hunny, by all means, invite *me*.

Policing The Area

As you may recall, I have a decided enjoyment of leftovers as a food group, and good reception leftovers would certainly be an exceptional treat in my estimation. But one must wait until they actually *become* left over. Not only must the scavenging wait until *all* of the guests have finished eating and relinquished their empty plates, it is preferable for scavengers to wait until *all* guests have vacated the premises so the scavengers might avoid the *appearance* of being what they truly are.

Queen CeeCee reports on the highlight of one reception she attended in her hometown: While the party was in full swing, with people still *chewing* their wedding cake, the mother of the groom was skulking about the tables with *fake* Tupperware containers, raking in mounds of finger food—sammiches, hunks of cheese, assorted nuts and mints—and working her way steadily to the cakes. She didn't go so far as to take food off the plates of the guests, but many were deprived of seconds or even firsts on many of the menu items. I scolded CeeCee for sitting in such obvious judgment of the groom's mama; perhaps, I told her, she was making a little care package for a poor, sick relative who couldn't make it to the festivities, being laid-up and all with a terminal *tapeworm*. Properly chagrinned at her hasty prejudice, CeeCee asked for forgiveness on the spot.

For those of you who are concerned about retrieving edible leftovers, CeeCee suggests just laying out the food in Tupperware containers to begin with. (It comes in practically every color in the *world*, you know, so there should be no problem matching it to your bridal color palette.) You can just put the lids (they burp for freshness!) underneath each container, so as soon as the door closes behind the last guest, your designated scavenger can swoop in and pop those lids on, give 'em a quick burp, and tote 'em on outta there, bigger'n Dallas. No pesky silver bowls and platters to wash, and the precious cargo can move directly to the refrigerator or freezer, transition to the microwave when necessary, and *"voy-ola"* (Y'allbonics for *voilà*), go right back to being a serving dish when snack time rolls around. Man, I wish I had invented Tupperware! I'd be having me some *fine* plastic surgery, I don't mind telling you.

Daincin' and Carryin' On

You gotta have loud music at your reception if you want people to dance and carry on, and of course, you do want that, because the retelling of it all is the most entertaining part of the whole wedding reception process. You'll want some good stuff that doesn't require too terrible much embellishment to make it worth hearing. If the music is loud enough, guests won't be able to talk to one another—or *you*—and they will be forced to dance and carry on.

"Dance and carry on" is a unified activity when alcohol is

involved. If drunk folks commence to *daincin'*, it's only a matter of moments before they also commence carryin' on. "Carryin' on" is any behavior that, when described, elicits heavy eye-rolling, head-clasping or -smacking, hand-wringing, hog-snorting, nose-spewing, pants-wetting, and belly-laughing from your audience right from your opening line ("Hunny, you ain't gon' be-*leeve this* shit!"). Your top-quality carryin' on necessitates a good relationship with a reliable, round-the-clock bail bondsperson, but make sure that at least one of his or her employees stays by the phone at work and isn't daincin' and carryin' on at your reception. Otherwise, who you gonna call? If you happen to be friends with any prominent judges in your area, it never hurts to have them in attendance, on account of you just never know.

In nearly every other situation requiring music, I vote for a real-live, in-person band, but I gotta tell you, I'm against hiring actual musicians for your wedding reception. For the best stories and photos, you need to target the absolute lowest common denominator in your guest list. That means having, of course, the Electric Slide, the Macarena, the Hokey Pokey, and what would *any* party worthy of note be without the Chicken Dance?

Ah yes, the Chicken Dance. Who *did* think up the Chicken Dance? What a choreographic sight to behold: four "squawks" with your hands as beaks, four "wing flaps" with your arms, four "chicken squats" involving booty-shaking and trying not to fall over, and then the big climax of four "hand claps," which requires you to bring *both* of your hands *together* in front of your body in an abrupt, repetitive fashion, thus producing that distinctive "clap" sound. After a brief bout of circular, arm-linked group trotting, it all begins *again* and, well, it's just awesome to see. And to be a *part* of it . . . Nobody forgets their first Chicken Dance, I can tell you that, or even their most recent.

The absolute *dumbest* guest can successfully perform these dance maneuvers. An absence of anything rhythmlike is an actual advantage—at least for the spectators. The brighter bulbs in your guest box will want to be moving around to avoid having to speak with the dumb ones, so pretty soon everybody's on the dance floor daincin' and headin' inexorably toward carryin' on. And *this* precludes your hiring a real-live, in-person *band* because no self-respecting, real-live, in-person band will *play* that crap.

10

The Wedding of the Century

Okay, I promised to tell you about how TammyCynthia came to be writing that very fine prenup for TammyMelanie and Sugar Bear. This also shows that it really doesn't take a year or a screaming fortune to have the Perfect Wedding if you get your mind right. It came to pass that the wise and wonderful and very good-looking Kathy Potts told Tammy-Melanie that on the upcoming Friday night she (Kathy) would hand-deliver a perfectly fabulous man to TammyMelanie for her blind-dating purposes, and that she (Kathy) thought he was worth some very careful consideration.

And so it was that TammyMelanie met Steven, who after some very careful consideration by TammyMelanie and the rest of us was deemed worthy of a helluva lot more than just careful *consideration*, if you catch my drift. Steven was determined to be Perfect in Every Way, and we *loved* him. That actually became and continues to be our mantra where he is concerned. Whenever a Steven-related tale is told, it's always followed by, "We *love* him." Some think that's his last name even. Steven We*love*him. So ooey-gooey was all Steven-related conversation that the Cutest Boy in the World said the guy's name oughta be Sugar Bear. And so we had it legally changed. It now says Sugar Bear on his driver's license even. (Well, I made up that last part, but the rest of it's true, I swear.)

Anyway, fortuitously for *him*, Sugar Bear found our TammyMelanie to be every bit as captivating as she did him, and so they fell in mad, passionate love with each other. (This makes them both a whole lot more pleasant to be around.) So, then, after a bunch of happy time passed, it was agreed by all (first of all by them, but very quickly by all of us, which was just as important) that the two of them should get married. Well, naturally, all the Queens and George could think of was "What are we going to wear to the wedding?" We began gleefully planning our outfits, only to have our hopes *cruelly* dashed when Tammy-Melanie informed us that she and Sugar Bear would be going on vacation—*without us*—to Key West, in April of 2005, and they would just offhandedly and, without our assistance and/or participation, get married while they were there, and furthermore, not only were we *not invited*, we were *expressly forbidden* from coming down there on our own. Well . . . I don't have to go into detail describing how we felt about *that* news, do I?

We let TammyMelanie know the length and depth and breadth and strength of our unhappiness with this arrangement, but she was adamant. If she had *us* there, she'd have to have *everybody* there, and she didn't *want* everybody there. To which we naturally replied that *we* didn't want everybody there, *either*. *That* was perfectly understandable, but we definitely wanted *us* there. A group pout ensued.

Then everything in the world came to one of those halts that screeches. Three weeks before their planned trip to Key West, I was in Little Rock, Arkansas, and my cell phone rang. The call was from TammyMelanie's home number and this was a weekday, so I knew *something* was wrong because Tammy-Melanie had *invented* "work ethic" and a call from home on a workday spelled trouble in my mind.

"What's wrong?" I asked, skipping right over the "hello" part.

"I have breast cancer," she said.

And with those words, everything in life changed for TammyMelanie and all of us who love her so dearly. The focus of everything changed in an instant. In 1962, Mary Jean Irion wrote about regular life in an essay entitled "Let Me Hold You While I May." It makes me cry every time I read it, but I love it anyway. See if it doesn't make you snivel just a little:

Normal day, let me be aware of the treasure you are. Let me learn from you, love you, savor you, bless you before you depart. Let me not pass you by in quest of some rare and perfect tomorrow. Let me hold you while I may, for it will not always be so. One day, I shall dig my nails into the earth or bury my face in the pillow or stretch myself out or raise my hands to the sky and want, more than all the world, your return.

We all take so for granted our regular ole normal days of living, and it all just turns on a blessed dime, I swear. One minute we were laughing and being happy for her and Sugar Bear, the next minute we were pissed off because they were going off to get married without us, and the *next* minute we were slammed, stunned and silent, against the wall by two little words, *breast cancer.*

But that was just for a minute. Anybody who thinks that part lasted more than a minute has *clearly* never met our TammyMelanie, who is just a bit on the competitive side. Meaning that, no matter what is going on, it *will* involve a heavy dose of her beating the dog shit outta *some*body at *some*thing. And she, thankfully, doesn't much care *what.* So, in very short order, she re-ordered her thinking to segue from shock, devastation, and fear right on into being the World Champion Chemo Patient and whipping the crap out of this cancer that had *dared* to venture into her beautiful bosoms. TammyMelanie hoards most of the world's supply of WhupAss, and she unleashed it.

We all rallied around her with offers of praying, hand-holding, meal-preparing, clothes-washing, house-cleaning, wig-buying, and transportation, as well as the thrashing of any individuals, family members or otherwise, who needed it. I offered to accompany her to chemo treatments, or "happy hour," as she called it, and observe the other patients. If anybody appeared to be getting ahead of her in any way, my job would be to try to demoralize them in order to make sure she kept that much-desired edge. In other words, humor was a primary weapon, in her arsenal for this fight. Thank God.

Okay, so her spirits and the troops were rallied. With the vacation/elopement plans shelved in order to focus on winning the Chemo Wars, TammyMelanie and Sugar Bear's marriage became of paramount importance to the two of them, while the actual wedding itself became merely problematic. How and when to accomplish the simple task of getting married? All TammyMelanie knew was what all she couldn't or didn't want to do. She was rendered just plain muddle-headed by all the medical crap that had taken over her formerly easygoing life and the whole getting married thing was fast becoming a huge *deal* in her mind. This was troublesome to the rest of us because we did not want our TammyMelanie to be having *any deals* in her life to fret over at this point. She needed to focus on winning them Chemo Wars.

She didn't want to just go to the courthouse, Sugar Bear's priest was out of town, and she hadn't had time to hunt down somebody else from her own church to perform the ceremony. Whenever she thought about adding anything to her to-do list, she just swooned. And the thought of her being in a swoon made all of us swoon, so all we had was a whole lot of swoonin' going on and not much of anything productive. We were all hanging back, not wanting to pester her with suggestions of potential solutions. For your future reference: Swooning individuals are not particularly receptive to suggestions of any kind.

The Chemo Wars were due to start the next week, and she didn't want to delay so long she'd have to get married bald. We figgered that on Sugar Bear's next day off, they'd just suck it up and go to a justice of the peace and get themselves married, and we resigned ourselves to not attending. Well, *some* of us resigned ourselves, but at least *one* of us had not, could not, and would not resign *shit*.

That would be me. So I decided, Fine, if she won't let us come to her ole wedding, I'll just have my *own* wedding for them and surprise them with it. My plan was to have them perform the time-honored African and Celtic tradition of "jumping the broom." In this ancient wedding ritual, the couple holds hands and jumps over a broom to signify leaving the carefree single life behind and going together into the bonds and responsibilities (and drudgery?) of the married state—the sweeping out of the old and in with the new, and all that.

A plan was percolating. Every day I'd tell TammyMelanie we all wanted to get together with her and Sugar Bear before she started the Chemo Wars, and she should just let me know when was good for her. Since none of the rest of us currently *has* breast cancer, I explained, we ain't got *shit* to do, comparatively speaking, and we'll adjust our schedules to suit hers at a moment's notice. Happy to do it. Finally, early on the morning of Wednesday, April 27, 2005, TammyMelanie announced that This Was the Day: She and Sugar Bear were available that evening to come over and have burgers with us. Okay, great, I said, sounding casual, but desperate to get her off the phone so I could set the wheels of my master plan in motion.

Naturally, my first call was to my Precious Darlin' George. (If an event calls for spontaneous decorating, he has got to be your first call.) He agreed to meet me at our lake house when he got off work. Wearing my workout clothes but not bothering to work out first, I hit the ground running and did not stop all day long until I had assembled the necessary tools for throwing a surprise "wedding." From my car, I called Cakes and Candles in Ridgeland, Mississippi, knowing that, by the end of this day, *I* at least would be wantin' some yummy cake, and plenty of it. They were admittedly a little surprised that I wanted a wedding cake for that same day, but when I explained the situation—the Chemo Wars about to commence and all—they jumped on the project with all four feet and vowed to put every wedding-y accoutrement they could find on that cake. I assured them that, in this case particularly, there was just no such thing as "too much crap" and exhorted them to pile it on. They were pretty excited by the time we hung up.

By the end of that call, I had arrived at my most important stop: David's Bridal, of course! Having had such good luck finding a dress off the rack for my ownself there, I hoped that fortune would grin at me once again. David did not disappoint. There was a whole rack of prom dresses marked half-price. I found TammyMelanie a very lovely white spaghetti-strapped dress with little silver stars all over it for fifty bucks. Then I found Sugar Bear a *truly hideous* "Mexican wedding–type" shirt, made from some unpronounceable synthetic that was sure to be hotter and more skin-searing and sweat-retentive than a genuine plastic bag. The store gave me a certificate that would entitle the bearer to a 10 percent discount on the next five-hundred-dollar purchase; I hung on to that, knowing that Sugar Bear would for sure want to buy some *more* ugly plastic clothes for hisownself.

Next, I went to Organizers in Highland Village (our favorite shopping center) and bought the cutest broom you ever saw in your life. Then I gathered up every piece of white paper wedding-type decoration in town, and I headed out to the lake.

At that point I called TammyMelanie's darlin' daughter, Amy, and after swearing her to secrecy, invited her to come to the double-secret surprise Jumping the Broom ceremony for her mom and Sugar Bear. I instructed her to swear in and invite TammyMelanie's own mother, whose name is Mary but we call her Murry, and she said she'd handle it all. I explained that I'd casually suggest to TammyMelanie that she bring Amy and Murry along to our burger party. Amy would inform Murry that, when invited, they should hesitate but then acquiesce, as if they were doing her a favor by coming along, but what the hell, they gotta eat *something*.

By this time, it was like five P.M. and they were coming over around seven. TammyCynthia had two jobs in the whole deal—well, she had three, but she claims she only *knew* about two of them. She only performed one and that took three tries. *One* of her jobs was to keep it a secret—which she *claims* she was totally unaware of, but thank God, she didn't have occasion to speak to TammyMelanie on the phone that day or she'da blabbed bigger'n Dallas, and I'd a killed her for sure. Next, she was to bring our present for TammyMelanie, a pink (of course) iPod with several thousand songs recorded on it, for use during the great Chemo Wars. She was also to go by my mailbox and pick up the "wedding music" CD, put it on her *own* iPod, and bring it and her little sound system so we could have the Wedding March and dance music for the post-jump party. Okay, four jobs—but she still only did one. She was supposed to be there by six to help decorate. She didn't even get home from work until six, and she kept leaving the house to come over, and she'd call about one thing or another, and I'd ask if she had the iPod, and she'd say, "Shit!" and turn around and go back to get it. Then she'd get in her house and get distracted and get something else, not the iPod, and head back over, calling *again* about something, and I'd ask *again* had she gotten the iPod and she'd go, "Shit!" and turn around again. She finally got there about 7:15, befuddled by my frantic behavior, and that's when we established that she *had no idea* this whole thing was supposed to be a surprise. She had, in fact, finally brought the iPod for TammyMelanie, but she had forgotten to pick up the CD and record it. If I'd had an extra few minutes to burn, I would have used them to maim, if not kill her, but it was not to be, and later on I was glad about that. I've known and loved her for more than thirty years, and this was hardly the first time she'd exhibited overt squirreliness, nor will it likely be the last.

A few minutes later, when TammyMelanie rolled into the driveway with Sugar Bear, Amy, and Murry, they were greeted by all of us, grinning over-widely, and the sight of big white paper wedding bells on *everything* from the mailbox on. The front door was covered up in bells and garlands and tassels and hearts, and the air was filled with massive quantities of bubbles (tiny ones) churned out by my new bubble machine.

Met by even *more* white crap festooning every surface, the guests of honor made their way into the keeping room, where all things white had come home to roost on the candlelit, white-light-laden table that held the wedding cake. When Tammy-Melanie and Sugar Bear admitted their confusion, I explained that while they would, in fact, get some burgers later on, *first* they would be getting "married" by jumping this darlin' broom (yet another thing that George had adorned with tons of frilly white shit). I had wanted to include "something blue" on the broom and then decided, for some reason that seemed logical to me at the time but eludes me now, that it needed to be a *bluebird*. Well, try to find a stuffed bluebird on short notice is all I'm saying. I musta gone to a hundred places looking for some semblance of a bluebird to put on that broom. What I finally *did see* was a little blue stuffed Dumbo the elephant, and so I snatched him up, thinking, What the hell, he's blue and he flies—he's a fucking bluebird in my book. So the broom had all manner of white ribbons and bows and bells and flowers, and a blue Dumbo smack dab in the middle of all of it.

The wedding cake ladies had worked themselves into a veritable froth with our cake. They had spared no effort nor inch of cake surface. It had columns and flowers (red, even—I told her we weren't real concerned with the virginal aspects of the whole thing) and bells and the mandatory little plastic bride and groom. As an extra-special added attraction, Cinderella's carriage, complete with white horses, careened across the top of the cake, and a big clock showed five minutes to midnight on the side of the cake. It was a vision of cakeliness, let me tell you.

George and Kyle, the Cutest Boy in the World, were snapping pictures, and we were all looking *so fine*, don'tcha know. I still had on the same twenty-year-old, raggedy Umbro shorts and prehistoric T-shirt I'd worn all day. TammyMelanie and TammyCynthia were similarly dressed, and there was not ten cents' worth of makeup on our collective faces.

I gathered up the girls in the party, and we all trooped upstairs to help the bride dress. Sugar Bear was herded off to don his "wedding shirt" and an enormous boutonniere George had constructed. All the guys were to gather at the foot of the stairs and await our dramatic descent. TammyCynthia's husband, Joe, and Kyle received their wedding baseball caps to wear: an orange Home Depot Racing Team cap and a Dale Earnhardt one. (Of course, they both whined and wanted the

Home Depot hat and we had to intervene and get them to agree to take turns.)

TammyCynthia and George and I were the bridesmaids, and we wore these little headband things I found that had pink sparkly crowns attached at the top and some very curly blond hair coming off the sides. Amy was the maid of honor, and her headband bore a giant multicolored butterfly. Murry had to double up and serve as both mother of the bride *and* best man, but hey, she was up for the job. Her headpiece was dignified, as warranted by her two important positions—a single extremely large felt rose.

Upstairs in the bride's room, along with the lovely white prom gown with the tiny sparkly stars were my *jumbo* light-up bouquet, which George had made for the goofy portion of my own wedding, and my twenty-foot veil, another George production. There was also a special-edition *Bride's Bible*, featuring many illustrations, including one or two on the cover, by Thomas Kincade, known as the Painter of Light. The traditional garter and an enormous rhinestone choker awaited our "bride." You'll recall that at my wedding, Melanie's tacky Southern Belle dress was the only one that had the choker feature, and she *loved* it, and we frankly have yet to hear the end of that *fucking* choker. So *fine*, we got her one. (She now has it out on permanent display at her home, and visitors all have to hear about it every single time they come to see her.)

At any rate, the dress fit perfectly, and her black flip-flops were just the right finishing touch for her bridal ensemble. She had, predictably, started sniveling upon first sight of the wedding decorations and by this time she'd worked herself up into a pretty good crying jag. We flipped part of the veil over her face, which enhanced the virginal effect of the whole thing and had the added benefit of muffling the sound of her sniveling.

The guys were all assembled at the foot of the stairs as, one by one, we, her attendants, made our way down. We all then hummed the Wedding March, since *somebody*—let's just call her *TammyCynthia* for short—forgot the *music*. We all hummed it in different keys and at varying tempos, but still our radiant bride floated down the staircase to meet her groom.

We then forced them to listen to the reading of the prenup TammyCynthia had prepared, and they agreed to all the terms. We had them sign on the dotted lines and we witnessed and whereas'd it to make it official. (It turned out that Tammy-Cynthia had misspelled Sugar Bear's last name, so he's got himself a loophole right there if he ever wants one.) I then handed them the vows I'd prepared for them and escorted them out to the patio, where the broom was lying in wait to be jumped.

Just as the sun set over the lake, they held hands and read their prepared vows (they swore to love and love *on* each other as much as either one of them could possibly stand *forever*). They walked around the broom three times, holding hands and carrying the special-edition *Bride's Bible.* And then they jumped over the broom together and we pronounced them *married* and sent Kyle off to cook the burgers—which was the only reason they thought they were invited to begin with. We drank a bottle of Dom and laughed and sniveled, and were just about as happy as any of us could ever remember being.

TammyMelanie remarked that she just wished it was *real*. She still just couldn't figure out how to make it happen or even *how* she wanted it to happen. Well, she said it two or three times during dinner, and finally I turned to her and said, "Now, are you *serious*? Because if you *are*, we can *get* a judge over here. No problem." She just lit up and said, *"Do it!"* And we said, "Do we need to ask Sugar Bear if he's in favor of it or just give him another beer and proceed?" We did both and he said he had the license in the car, where he'd been riding around with it for the last *month*, trying to get her to marry him. We *love* him.

So TammyCynthia—who's known and admired by every judge in the state—picked up her cell phone and commenced calling up judges. The very first one she called, Judge Harold McCarley, said, sure, he'd be right on over, be glad to do it. We weren't surprised. After all, it was only ten-thirty. You know he was just sittin' there, waitin' for somebody to call him up and ask him to get dressed and drive twenty-five miles out to a lake to marry some folks who were in a big hurry.

My daughter, Bailey, called and we told her what was about to happen and she hauled ass out there. We were not fooled— she thought we had more Dom—but we were glad to have her there under any pretenses. Shortly afterward, His Honor showed up in the appropriate Hawaiian shirt and we assured him that the bourbon supply was intact, should he find himself in need of refreshment after he performed his duties.

The Wedding of the Century

At 11:15 P.M., Kyle went out and lit candles all over the deck that sticks out over the water, and we all trooped out there and had us a bona fide wedding. TammyMelanie and Sugar Bear repeated the vows I'd written for them, and the judge had them say some other stuff, and the geese were honking in the distance as he pronounced them really and for true, husband and wife.

It was far and away the best and happiest wedding I have ever seen. We all just cried and grinned for days and days afterward. None of us could believe it had really happened. I mean, they came for burgers and went home married. And, of course, the very best part of the whole thing is: *I got to go to the wedding after all*—so HA!

Important Note: I am thrilled to report that TammyMelanie is the Reigning World-Champion Chemo Patient. She is cancer-free, feeling fine, looking even finer, and Sugar Bear has lived to tell the tale. All is well—Hallelujah Jesus!

The Newlywed Kit

The first time I got married was in, uh, lemme see, 1978, I believe. We got the blood tests and they gave me my first Newlywed Kit. Yes, it comes in a preprinted, sealed bag that says *Newlywed Kit* right on it, and it was 100 percent free to anybody getting a blood test prior to getting married. I could hardly wait to *see* the essentials for starting our new life together. The only item I can recall was a sample of Massengill douche. I was insulted at the time and I remain insulted to this day.

The *next* time I got married was in 1987, and I'd say it was a good thing that no makers of knives, guns, or poisons had seen fit to offer free samples of their wares in that particular edition of the Newlywed Kit. If they'da put in a small chainsaw and some Hefty bags, the words you're now reading would no doubt have been written on the jailhouse wall instead of in this very fine book.

Clearly, the nice folks putting together all those free Newlywed Kits have never actually been married theirown-selves. They've got samples of breakfast cereal and detergent and fake Tupperware and deodorant, and they've got promotions for fancy stereos and cute checks with your new name on them. I'd like to see the kits some women who've *been* married might assemble. I think there'd be stuff like earplugs and weaponry and sales pitches from private detectives and tombstone engravers and samples of Xanax and an assortment of alcoholic beverages, for sure. And the names of some good vasectomists or not-so-good ones, even. Some snoring remedies—perhaps a really heavy pillow, for example? (I find that if you put one over his face and hold it there, the snoring stops.) Divorce attorneys are missing a prime advertising opportunity here, as are bail bondsmen. Alcohol and drug and debt counselors oughta be in there, too. Plastic surgeons could run a special on "boobs bigger and better than your husband's girlfriend's."

Many, *many* years passed before I was even able to think the *M* word again, but as you all know, by and by, I did meet, fall in love with, and deign to marry the Cutest Boy in the World, and I am thrilled to report that, at this writing, I am still glad about it all and, thankfully, haven't needed any of the above-mentioned items—yet. (Well, truth be told, there *was* some Pepto-Bismol in our kit, and I think we've both used it a time or two—but, as they say, shit *does* happen.)

But, hallelujah, sometimes we're lucky—blessed—enough to find ourselves in relationships where the problems aren't of the chainsaw-and-Hefty-bag variety—just a little Pepto every now and then. Hearing stories of Love Gone *Right* from fellow Queens played a big part in giving me the encouragement even to *think about* thinking about getting married again—even if he *was* the Cutest Boy in the World. I thank all you wonderful women for sharing your lives with me and giving me hope and the courage to try one more time.

When Queen Lori was dating her Spud Stud Dave, they talked about memorable childhood Christmases. Lori's most unforgettable one was when she was five and her favorite aunt sent her the nicest present she'd ever received—a china tea set from overseas. As her dad took a picture of her with her gift, her brother, trying to be helpful, pushed down on the box to keep it from blocking her face and smashed the whole brand-new china tea set to bits before she'd ever played with it once. Sad as her dairy-farming parents were, they were poorer still and couldn't afford to replace her treasure. (Bless her little heart. I know just how she felt, what with never getting any real majorette boots and all.) Well, the second Christmas she was married to her Darlin' Dave, he was off fighting a war in Iraq, but he somehow managed to get her a present, and he sent it with instructions not to open it until Christmas Day. Yes, he did what you think he did: Even in the midst of war, his thoughts were with her, of her, and the precious man sent her a little china tea set. Now, if that doesn't bring a tear to your eye, something is bad wrong with you is all I'm saying. Of course, it made me want to marry *Dave*, and that wasn't a good situation.

Hanah Louise and Charlie had dated for six years even though she had a fragile daughter with mountains of special medical needs, which would've sent most men running screaming for their lives. Charlie stayed. Right after her daughter had spinal surgery, Hanah Louise discovered she was pregnant. Charlie stayed. He asked her to marry him on Christmas Eve, slipping the ring into a book she'd asked for by cutting a hole in the pages without slicing a single word! Their daughter, Lilly, was born with severe food allergies—everything she ate caused her to bleed internally—and a life-threatening heart condition. Charlie stayed. Three days before their wedding, Lilly was rushed to the hospital for surgery. On her wedding day, Hanah Louise got dressed for the ceremony and they got married in the hospital chapel; her best friend came to sit with Lilly. The honeymoon was in the hospital. I now wanted to marry Charlie.

Then I read a piece in *Oprah* magazine by Gail Stocker, an interview with Mavis Leno, where she spoke about her marriage to Jay. Mavis talked about how supportive he was of her work to end the mistreatment of Afghan women, and it was wonderful to read what a great marriage they have. But what really spoke to me was the ending. Mavis said she didn't just *love* Jay, she was madly *in love* with him—and she was a person (like me) who'd never really believed it possible to sustain that feeling. She quoted a poem from the movie *Roman Holiday* that she used as a measure of whether or not she really loved someone or was just fooling herself: "If I were dead and buried, and I heard your voice, beneath the sod my heart of dust would still rejoice." If she were dead and Jay walked on her grave, she said "My heart would still dance. He is just all joy to me."

And I knew I felt that way about Kyle Jennings, and so I married him. My wish, my prayer for you—if you're considering marrying someone—is that you both have that feeling for each other. I'm pretty sure it's the only way it will work.

The

Sweet Potato Queens'
Divorce Guide

The Sweet Potato Queens'
Divorce Guide

Jill Conner Browne

Crown Publishers
NEW YORK

ISBN-13: 978-1-4000-4969-1
ISBN-10: 1-4000-4969-5

Printed in the United States of America

Design by Lynne Amft

To Frank Mastronardi—my beloved Mr. M—

with all my love and gratitude,

for teaching me to look for what would make my heart sing

CONTENTS

Contents

Statistically speaking, 100 percent of all divorces begin with weddings. If you're reading this section of the book first, you may be scared off from the idea of a wedding for the time being and not even want to turn this book over and read *The Wedding Planner.* If that happens, thank your lucky stars, on account of, if just *reading* about it scares you, Lord help you, the real thing would probably finish you off entirely. Marriage is daunting enough, but lemme tell you, *divorce* is just not for pussies. Divorce is the *easy* way out, they say. Ha! I think "they" are the ones locked into miserable marriages. Nothing about getting a divorce is easy, inexpensive, or painless. Change of any kind is hard for most of us, and we resist it with every fiber of our beings. We just want whatever it is to *go away* without fanfare and certainly without effort. Well, getting a divorce is gonna require some pretty major effort.

But fear not, my little chickens, the Sweet Potato Queens are here to assist and advise you. Believe me, we are well

qualified, having amongst us around thirteen marriages and eight divorces—so far—not to mention more than three hundred combined years of valuable experience, for which there is no substitute. And out of all that, I'm proud to say, there hasn't been one killing or even maiming—and we've had us some men who deserved both.

If you're new to the irreverent world of the Sweet Potato Queens, you need to know that there are four other books about our antics, which provide invaluable insights into how you should do just about everything in life. I know everything about everything. Well, truth be told, I don't *know* anything about anything. I just have an *opinion* about everything and, boy hidee, we have to say it is mine and mine alone—not shared by my editors, publishers, friends, or family. Nobody, including me, thinks you oughta do a *thing* I say in real life, except laugh a whole lot. We all agree you should do that.

From our humble beginnings in the 1982 St. Paddy's Parade in Jackson, Mississippi, to the Worldwide Order of Pie Kappa Yamma with chapters in over twenty countries (and counting), we are ever-growing, -extending, and -expanding our grasp and influence. We're also getting fatter by the minute from the recipes in these books, but it must be pointed out that there has been a corresponding improvement in our dispositions.

To discover and display to full advantage your own True Queenliness, we invite you to be in Jackson, Mississippi, the third weekend in March for the annual Mal's St. Paddy's Parade on Saturday (it doesn't matter *when* St. Patrick's Day actually is).

Yes, I mean it, and come visit our website at www.sweetpotato
queens.com and the Message Board of Love. You can even e-mail
me directly at hrhjill@sweetpotatoqueens.com with any and all
questions, and I'll answer them my very ownself. Sometimes it
takes me a while, but sooner or later you'll hear back from *me*,
not some lackey. (I don't have nearly enough lackeys to do the
things I *don't* want to do, so I certainly can't spare one to do
the stuff I purely love to do, which is to enlighten you with my
opinions.)

So come now and walk with us through the valley of the
shadow of divorce. Heeding our advice may help you avoid it
altogether. But if the worst comes, you'll learn in these pages
how to rise from the ashes and dance once more in the light of
your own soul and laugh right out *loud* about life itsownself.
And, hey, if you don't feel like laughing immediately, good news:
We got snacks in here that'll speed your recovery as only a little something sweet, salty, fried, or au gratin can.

The

Sweet Potato Queens'
Divorce Guide

1

Pre-D

Okay, so you know it's over. You're engaged to be divorced from your former fiancé and erstwhile groom. What shall we call him in polite company? TammyMelanie has her own word for *groom;* she calls him "the Gloom." I'm now declaring that henceforth the men we're legally hooked up with will be "grooms" until we decide to run them off. Thereafter they're "glooms." The corresponding title for the exiting bride will become "the Glide," because that's just we hope she does—glide right on out the door. We'll do our best to make that happen.

The first thing you need to know is this: It's way more trouble to get divorced than it is to get married. I would have to say that getting a divorce is comparable to having a wedding in terms of the time it usually takes—at least a year—and all the errand running involved. Now, I'd pretty much rather be set on fire than have to do a whole bunch of errands, so if you feel the same way, before you start down the road to getting a divorce, you need to be sure you have a good enough reason to warrant all those errands. Remember, just as having a wedding has nothing whatsoever to do with getting married, so it is that *getting* a divorce has nothing to do with *being* divorced. I myownself have been divorced a time or two and I do believe it can be a worthwhile venture. I'll try to help you make the "getting" part as smooth as possible.

Let's just say up front that whatever your reason(s) for the divorce, we understand completely and support you totally in your decision. And let's just clarify that *your* reasons don't have to be *our* reasons. What pushes you over the precipice might not even be a blip on our radar screen and vice versa. *You are the only one who truly needs to be comfortable with your choice.* Just as you may have been the only person in the universe who wanted you to marry the guy in the first place, you might also find yourself alone in the desire for a divorcement to take place. Nobody but you really knows what's been going on behind y'all's closed doors. That's mostly on account of we all try to hide our misery for so long before we admit to it, as if concealing it will make it go away. And if we've done a pretty good act-

ing job, other people may be genuinely surprised and confused when we announce our intention to divorce him so we can avoid having a murder conviction on our résumé. They thought, because we fooled them into it, that he was a perfectly nice man. (More on the "perfectly nice man" later.)

Before we get into the why's and how's of divorce, though, let me give you one strong word of caution, and I hope you'll hear me on this because this piece of advice alone is worth the price of this book: If you are even contemplating a divorce, *Don't do anything to your hair now!* Trust me on this.

It's just like when you're pregnant—you should *never* attempt a new hairstyle or color when you're expecting. For one thing, when you're pregnant, you have gobs more hair than you ever had before in your life, and it is *fabulous*—it is the hair of your dreams. And almost immediately postpartum, what doesn't fall out gets weird. I'm certain that this has been the *true* underlying cause of postpartum depression all along, but nobody else has figured it out. So there's no point in getting an extravagant new hairstyle for your fabulous new hair, because it has only been loaned to you by the universe for the duration of your pregnancy. It will be recalled the second you deliver, and your new hairstyle will be torn asunder—much like the rest of your life, actually, but that's another story.

When you are in the throes of divorce, the temptation to mess with your hair is nearly overwhelming. You must resist. YOU MUST. No hairstylist on earth can measure up or take the pressure of trying to fix your life by fixing your hair. And no

matter what fabulosity you walk out of the salon with, that creepy guy will *still be there*, in your house, in your life, bearing the title of "husband."

Good hair makes up for a lot, I suppose (I can *only* suppose, since I only have about four hairs on my head, and at least three of 'em are gray), but enviable as it may be, good hair does not a good life make. And it is an unassailable fact that no matter what you do to your hair when you are miserable, you will hate it, and that only serves to compound what was already a bad situation. You will still have the crappy husband and the unbearable situation to deal with, and now you have to face it all with an orange buzz cut. And that will distract you and needlessly delay the business at hand—that being that you need to get a divorce.

Your problem is not your hair. It's *him*. The sooner you face that reality, the sooner you will be divorced and ready for a new hairstyle that you will *love*. You'll be so euphoric about your life in general that it can't help but carry over into your beauty shop. Nothing, good or bad, happens in a vacuum.

We don't have the same rule about clothes that we have for hair. And we all know how much better we can *glide* with some new clothes. As soon as the idea of divorce crosses your mind, you should start planning and acquiring the new wardrobe you'll need for your fabulous new life. You can start with your outfits for Mal's St. Paddy's Parade Weekend. Oh, hunny, you've got to come. I'd venture to say being in Jackson, Mississippi, the third

weekend in March is almost a medical necessity for all Queens, but it's the healing equivalent of Lourdes for newly minted Glide Queens. It's the very best way to reintroduce yourself into society. Think of yourself as a debutante who's just a little bit on the trashy side. (There're lots of Glooms here, too, but they're somebody else's Glooms. And somebody else's Gloom just might be your Glee.)

One of the best and most entertaining parts of any occasion is The Outfit. The Sweet Potato Queens have created an outfit-rich environment for our subjects and fellow monarchs. Queens all over the world begin at least a year in advance planning outfits for Parade Weekend—and not just for the festivities themselves. Outfits are also needed for traveling *to* Jackson, so that not only can all the Queens easily recognize one another's true Queenliness but also and equally important, so that all innocent bystanders encountered along the way in rest stops, fast-food establishments, airports, and the like will *know* immediately and unquestionably that they are in the Presence of Royalty and ask to take photographs.

Queens like to arrive at the O-fficial SPQ Ho-tel, the Jackson Hilton, in a fair amount of regalia so that the staff knows to give them the Royal Treatment (and do they ever!) but also so that any other regular ole guests will know that when they check out and go on home, they are *so* missing out on the time of their lives. (The first year we were headquartered at the Jackson Hilton, a bunch of guys were checking out as the Queens started rolling in, and they were agog. They booked

rooms in advance for Parade Weekend the following year and have never missed a year since. Smart boys.) Outfits are needed for Thursday night at the Earlybird Welcome Festivities, and for the SPQ Luncheon on Friday at Bravo! you'll want an outfit with a *hat*.

Major outfits are desirable for the SPQ Ball on Friday night at Hal & Mal's, the O-fficial Watering Hole of the Sweet Potato Queens. In 2005 we were lucky enough to make the acquaintance of Anthony Richards, and Lord have mercy, the ballgowns that man made for us would make Barbie drool with envy. A worldwide sequin shortage was declared after he got through with those dresses. He's our new best friend, and he can be yours as well—just go look at his wares at www.sequinqueen.com. After the ball comes the After-Glow at the Hilton. Most of us change into something comfy for this 'cause we all be so tired.

Our Queenly participation in the annual Mal's St. Paddy's Parade on Saturday naturally requires our *most* major outfits. They always involve much sparkly stuff on account of the sun always shines on this parade, and there's nothing that will make you happier on this earth than blinding a bunch of spectators with your very own sequins. Parade outfits do not need to be especially comfy. It's way more important on public occasions such as this to *look* good than it is to *feel* good. (It does help, however, if one can pee without too much ado. Enough said.)

The parade turns into the street dance, and after *that*, it's time for "Pearls and PJ's" at the Hilton. Outfits for this event are

just what the name implies—jammies and joory. Thousands and thousands of darlin' women in an unbelievable array of "sleep-wear" will be dancing their collective asses completely *off* in the ballroom, in the halls, in the elevators, by the pool, in the coffee shop, and in the parking lot. We like to think of the whole week-end as a spring break for grown-ups. If there was a video, it'd be called *Middle-Aged Women Gone Wild*, or maybe *Old-Ass Women Gone Wild and a Whole Bunch of Too Gorgeous Young Things Gone Wild and the Men Who Loved Them All*.

The final event of the weekend is the SPQ Brunch at the Hilton, and nobody is very cute by this time. Precious few out-fits appear at this event; we're lucky people even bother to show up *dressed*. The brunch is the sweetest time of the whole week-end. We've all Queened ourselves slap to death for several days and nights, and now we're ready to sit down and have a big bowl of Brenda's Shrimp and Grits and just bask in our own glory for a spell. I usually speak for a little bit and Kacey Jones leads us in our "hymn," "Never Wear Panties to a Party." One year, as I stood in my closet trying to decide what to wear to the brunch, I was just overcome with "dog-ass tired" and couldn't bear the thought of any garment touching my flesh. I picked up my exquisitely soft chenille bathrobe—the one Queen TammyCarol had given me, with a big crown on the back—and my pink fuzzy slippers, and I put them on. Sighing a deep, contented sigh, I told the Cutest Boy in the World that I was ready to go. He looked per-plexed, but he instinctively determined that this was probably not the best moment to develop a sudden interest in fashion.

(He's not only the cutest, he's also the smartest.) Off we went to the Hilton.

When I arrived, the ballroom was filled with Queens awaiting shrimp and grits and looking just a wee bit mystified by the "outfit" I'd chosen. I stepped up to the microphone and said, "I know y'all are thinking there must be some fancy something-or-other underneath here and that I'm gonna suddenly whip off this bathrobe for the Big Reveal, but I ain't. I am absolutely eaten up with dog-ass tired, and this *is* my outfit." (By the way, we'll soon be offering Official SPQ Bathrobes so that we can all be comfy *and* matching for our future brunches.)

The outfits you'll need for your divorce are no less important than those for Parade Weekend, and planning them should be an equal source of entertainment for you. If you'll actually be forced to go into court to obtain your freedom, it's advisable to put together a sort of "poor, pitiful me" disguise. Think mousy brown, high-necked, long-sleeved, loose-fitting (although ill-fitting would be an added bonus), and well-worn. You want to look poor but proud. Sensible shoes are a must, and they should be obviously inexpensive and several years old. Your handbag should have a short handle, and you must clutch it primly in front of you. Keep your makeup to a minimum and your hairstyle simple. One step above Amish is what you're aiming for here.

You'll also want to practice looking meek and mild in front of a mirror. Depending on how long this divorce mess has dragged out, your disposition may be nearing wolverine status,

and that is just not a sympathy-invoking look to wear into divorce court. Since most of the players in this little drama are likely to be of the male persuasion, it will be extremely useful if you're also a master of the teary-eyed, trembly-chin thing. Most of them crumble in the presence of this demeanor regardless of any relevant facts suggesting that it is the facial equivalent of a bald-faced lie.

But what's that you say? That this is blatantly dishonest, utterly manipulative, and degrading to you as a highly evolved, self-actualized woman? Mmm-hmmm . . . And your point is? Look, all I'm saying is, I'm sure it's also embarrassing to the chameleon to be cowering on the garden wall, changing color all the time, trying so desperately to blend in. You know he'd rather get up on his hind legs and whip the shit outta that cat, but at the moment, the camouflage thing is the best weapon in his arsenal, and so he uses it. War is, in fact, still war, and winning is still the preferred outcome. So if a little totally fake teary-eyed, trembly-chin bullshit will get you what you need, I say, crank it on up, hunny. Just so long as *you* know it's just an act, that you really are *not* that pathetic teary-eyed, trembly-chinned creature you're portraying at the moment. This ruse should be used *only* as an absolute emergency-situation strategy and never allowed to become a life position or reflective of your own self-image.

As soon as the unpleasantness has passed and the court has ruled in your favor, you should excuse yourself to the nearest private location and morph into your New Self. He's the Gloom, and you're the Glide. You should feel, act, and look your

part. Now is the time for you to look your stunning best, which will make you feel fantastic, which will make you look even better—all of which will make him wretched, and this, in turn, will make you feel even better. My, what a happy circle!

I think our buddy Anthony Richards at www.sequinqueen .com oughta make a special Glide's dress for the newly divorced girl to wear to her divorce party. He and you can be really creative here, since there are no established guidelines. What is the Glide's equivalent of the Big JuJu Wedding Dress? This is your chance to be your most spectacular. Don't hold back. Go for a genuine work of art.

And while he's at it, our Anthony will be needing to make Glidesmaid dresses for all your best friends, which, unlike bridesmaid dresses, can be stunning in every respect. And the mother of the Glide needs something special to wear for the occasion as well. (Hellooo? Anthony? Are you paying attention?) I can just see the beautiful divorce party portraits in the divorce album on the coffee table.

And for the wonderful nights when you are *finally* blissfully alone in your own home—and believe me, you will come to treasure these nights as the gift they are—you must have some of our big, giant lolling panties. Go to www.sweetpotatoqueens.com and look at 'em and just *try* to imagine how comfy they are—you won't even come close, but just try. Picture it: just you, your big, giant lolling panties, Chocolate Stuff, and absolute power over the remote control. You must never tell your married friends about it, though. It's just too cruel.

2

The Moment of Truth

How come it is you're wanting this divorce in the first place? Every time I think I've heard every possible excellent reason, I am proven wrong. Smart, strong women tell me stuff every day, tales that will astound you. These are women who had their own personal lives so much together, you would have thought they were virtually asshole-proof. Let this be a dire warning to us all. If you think you're asshole-proof, don't get too cocky; somewhere out there there's probably a *bigger* asshole who wants you to share his name.

Oh, you'll let things rock on for a long time. You'll refuse to believe what you see and even refuse to believe what you feel. We all figure out how our lives *ought* to be, and try to make them into that, and it takes a good while sometimes before we come to our senses. We come up with excuses to continue believing that things ain't so bad and everything will work itself out. Eventually, however, there comes the Moment of Truth, when we finally see clearly enough to get off our asses and do something about it. That moment has many variations. Here's a small sampling of the possibilities that await the unwary:

A sweet girl from St. Louis cleaned out the closet she shared with her traveling-salesman rat-bastard of a husband and found two receipts for items she never personally received—a very expensive designer purse and an *abortion*. Most of her first alimony check went to procure just such a gen-u-ine designer purse for herownself. She feels good all over every time she carries that purse. We're not surprised. It makes us happy and proud just hearing about it.

Then there's Queen Linda's daughter, never one to snoop, who looked in her husband's Day-Timer once, at his request, to get some information he needed. She couldn't help noticing that he had a busy day planned for the following Wednesday, when he had himself scheduled, in one day, *in this order*, to (1) take the dog to the groomer and (2) see a divorce attorney. Well, how do you do! I guess we all have our priorities. Thankfully, when the dust settled, she only had to live with the *one* dog, the four-legged one.

Queen Scout was initially distraught when she discovered that some time ago, her beloved, totally unbeknownst to her had also become the beloved of another woman, who just happened to reside in a mobile home. "The thought of takin' a can opener to her trailer did cross my mind," Scout said. "And then it dawned on me: 'For *what*? To get a turd back? That is her problem!' " Eggzackly.

Sometimes the moment of truth is especially painful because you know you should have known from the start. There are just some people you have to stay clear of. This bit of advice from our Homecoming Queen and TammyPippa: They point out that if any member of your beloved's family is a certifiable freeze-dried wackaloon, then it is probably only a matter of time before said beloved begins to exhibit similar behaviors.

Queen TammyAnn Tootacky found this to be true in the person of her ex. Although he had felt no particular compunction to shell out any U.S. dollars to help defray the expenses of their mutual daughter's wedding, he did so graciously offer to *perform* at the reception. He wanted to play his guitar and sing for the couple's first dance. They agreed, albeit with a fair amount of trepidation and reservations on the part of the mother of the bride.

TammyAnn is nobody's fool and certainly not *this* guy's, so she made arrangements with her partner in Queenly crimes, Anita Piece, to start yanking plugs out of amplifiers should the "performance" run over. It did and she did. Further attempts to take the stage during the band's breaks were similarly thwarted

by the two. TammyAnn would like you to remember *before* you marry up with any potential freeze-dried wackaloons that they likely won't improve any with age, and probably, if only out of perversity, they'll manage to live long enough to be an embarrassment at your daughter's wedding.

Queen Cherry thought she was doing her friend Karen a big favor when she fixed her up on a blind date with a rich guy named Harry. Cherry didn't know Harry all that well, but she did know he was rich as *all get out* (translation for Yankees: rich as shit), and so she and Karen both figured how bad could he be, right? Well, Karen called Cherry as soon as she got home after that first date and reported that Harry had taken her to a fancy-pants restaurant for dinner, where he proceeded to drink his soup directly from the bowl without benefit of spoon. Now, this was somewhat off-putting to our Karen, but the romance continued and found them engaged six months later, and soon after that, they were married. But she divorced him a year later because she simply could not tolerate his abominable manners, table and otherwise, any longer. Money, even large sums of it, is no substitute for knowing how to act when you get somewhere. And this is just proof of what I am always saying—if you don't like something they do *before* you marry 'em, you're gonna not like it a whole lot more after you do.

Of course, there's also the possibility (it *does* happen) that he is a Perfectly Nice Man and you are a hound from hell and just find him boring. I knew a young woman who found herself in just such a situation, and she was in a quandary as to just how

she was gonna convince her mama that she had to have this divorce. Her mama looooved her Perfectly Nice son-in-law, and Little Missy knew that unless she came up with something pretty dang convincing, *she* was likely to be the one missing Thanksgiving dinner at Mama's house in the future.

She conferred with her sister, and they racked their brains for a reason that would be acceptable to Mama but also absolutely guarantee that Mama wouldn't try to discuss it with the future ex and have the whole big lie explode. Well, they came up with just the thing, which they knew their mama would be categorically against: anal sex. Little Missy would tell her mama that beneath that Perfectly Nice Man's exterior beat the heart of a butt-fucking fiend.

Oh, she hemmed and hawed and tippy-toed around the subject for the better part of an hour, trying to just *imply* it, in the hopes that she wouldn't have to tell an out-and-out bald-faced lie to her mama about a person who was just a Perfectly Nice, albeit terminally boring, man. But Mama just wasn't getting it. I imagine it would be a difficult conversational inference for Mama to make, so far removed was it from her own personal sphere of experience as to be practically unknown and certainly un*heard* of. And surely nobody Mama knew would ever discuss such a thing, since to do so would necessitate admitting that one even knew about it. But Little Missy labored on with her leading references and delicate implications and Mama continued to look bewildered.

Finally, frustrated and desperate to end this conversation,

Little Missy just blurted out, "I'm talking about anal sex, Mother! That is *all* he ever wants to do, and he wants to do it all the time! I have taken it up the butt for that man so many times, I cannot stand it anymore. I'm afraid if I stand in a draft, I'll sound like a goddamn jug band!"

The perfectly nice son-in-law was summarily divorced and remains to this day blissfully unaware of the besmirchment of his good name and proclivities. Little Missy and her equally wicked sister enjoyed many a chuckle over the years—at their mama's house for Thanksgiving dinner. All's well that ends well and all that. (But don't you just wonder what Mama told her lady friends?)

Divorce is grossly underappreciated as a source of hilarity, in my opinion. You *will* have fond memories of your divorce—I promise—and quite possibly more than you had from the wedding and marriage. Really, if it wasn't so great, do you think it would be so popular? Think about it.

My friend Tomboy was stunned when her ex made his departure from their marital home. She was shocked on two accounts: first of all, because nobody had ever left *her* before—she'd always done any necessary leaving herownself—and, second, because he left Jenny behind. Jenny was his Great Dane. When Tomboy called friends to tell them what had happened, the universal response was, "My God! I cannot believe he left Jenny!" Tomboy was somewhat miffed that none of them expressed any

surprise at his leaving *her*, but being a much better person than any of her friends could ever hope to be, she forgave them.

But anyway, a few weeks after he left, the low-life dog-abandoner returned. After a number of unsuccessful attempts at using his key in the lock (she really is a tomboy and changed all the locks herownself quicker'n shit through a goose as soon as he drove out of sight that first night), he gave up and rang the bell. When she opened the door, he reached out and attempted to pet Jenny, who, doing a remarkable imitation of her mistress, I imagine, sat back on her haunches and growled her greeting at him. The ex slunk off in abso-*lute* rejection and Tomboy and Jenny went out for cheeseburgers. I just love me a good dawg story, don't you?

A reader from Chicago wrote me about a touching classified ad in the newspaper where a woman was selling her ex-husband's casket—who, it should be noted, had not had the decency to die as yet. "Marriage died before husband did," the notice said. Apparently, the woman planned to be cremated, but the ex wanted a traditional burial and a friend of theirs had snagged the casket for 'em at his metal-salvage business. The woman looked upon it as a good investment for the future, and even though her husband didn't obligingly *die* and use the thing, she was able to sell it to cover some of her attorney's fees.

Our very own RedQueen divorced a particularly unsavory character who, sometime down the road, had gotten about three years in arrears (or, as we say Down Here, "in the rear") on his child-support payments when he up and got a promotion at

work that put him in the position of chasing down deadbeat dads for nonpayment of child support! I'm not making this up. And he actually delivered this news to her himself. She stood there, looking no doubt as flabbergasted as she truly was that not only would he be hired for such a duty but that he could bring himself to admit it out loud to her and their then-five-year-old daughter. Puzzled by her mother's look and silence, the child asked, "Mommy, what does that mean?" RedQueen turned to her little girl and said the only thing she really could say: "Hunny, it just means that God has got a terrific sense of humor."

I heartily agree and add the good news is that He also pays attention. This proves it: Queen Jennifer had been married to a man so abusive she had to get a restraining order against him to make sure she even survived the divorce. They had a construction business, but it apparently slipped his mind that it was all in her name. When she went to court to get the restraining order, she fired his ass and handed him his termination letter and final check right on the spot. She's still kicking herself for not taking a photographer with her to court that day. A picture of the look on his face would have been a lifetime treasure. As it was, though, her good friends had a copy of the termination letter framed for her, and it hangs in the office she no longer has to share with his sorry ass.

3

On Matters Legal
and Mannerly

Just about anybody can perform
a wedding ceremony that will be
virtually indistinguishable from any other
wedding ceremony in its result. If our very
own Jay Sones, who mail-ordered and
received his O-fficial Preacher Certificate
without benefit of having attended one
single solitary seminary-type class or
even seminar (although it must be
noted he *did* attend, under extreme
duress, every available class and/or
service at Northminster Baptist
Church in Jackson, Mississippi,

from birth until around age eighteen, and he can recite any number of "memory verses" right off the top of his head to this very day), marries you to some other person, you are every bit as legally bound to them as if you stood up in the Vatican and got hitched up by the pope hisveryownself, even though Jay ain't no more a preacher than the Geico lizard.

Okay, so that's all fine for getting married, but you're gonna want to be a little more choosy about your selection of divorce attorneys. If you were broke when you got married and you're broker still now and nobody owns a friggin' thing and there are no children involved, then it's not gonna matter a whole lot who handles the paperwork for you. (Just make sure, for future reference, that you do end up with a little blue folder from the state that declares that you are actually *divorced*.)

If, on the other hand, there are any marital assets at stake and you want to end up with any of 'em, it behooves you to learn the name of the biggest-dick divorce attorney in town— and hire him or her *first*. Go by for a chat. Even if you can't afford to use him or her yourself, this will fix it so your soon-to-be-ex can't hire 'em to use against you. If there is any dick-wielding to be done in this deal, you want to be the wielder not the wieldee.

The assets don't have to range in the big figures to be important enough for a good lawyer. When Queen Debi was trying to get divorced from Fred, he just kept getting pettier and pettier about the whole thing, especially regarding what all he wanted to keep out of the deal. He was particularly wound

up over his *hand truck*—also known in most circles as a dolly. Our Goddess of the Blues had her attorney specify in the decree that "Fred can have his dolly back." Made him look real butch.

Hire a good (read: mean-ass) lawyer and pay attention to what they tell you. Mind 'em. This is bidness (or "business" in other parts) and it's *their* bidness. So let them do what they do best, which is getting you legally parted from that other person and covering your ass while they do it. They ain't marriage counselors or psychologists. Their job is to get you out of this mess, not clean it up.

As I said earlier, God *does* pay attention, as a friend of ours discovered when she finally dragged her pitiful self to the divorce attorney's office and began the process that had been inevitable in all her friends' minds since the wedding day. Her tough lady lawyer kindly sat her down and began getting the details of the situation that rendered her services necessary. They got to "name" on one of the forms and our friend supplied the given name of the asshole in question. The lawyer jerked her head up, put down her pen, and said, "Do you mean that little short prick who's a cop over in Such-and-Such County who struts around like he is God's gift to women *and* law enforcement?" "Uh-huh." The lawyer's face broke into a beatific grin, and she said, "Ma'am, it will be a pure pleasure to take on your case. I hate his guts." It was as if the heavens opened and the room filled with light; a choir of angels sang, and there was great rejoicing.

That mean little lawyer got hold of his ass, and she hung on like a cross between a snapping turtle and a pit bull, and she didn't quit until she had that cop signed up for alimony until the end of time, and lots and lotsa child support until the last one was twenty-one. We have nominated that lawyer for sainthood and we're still waiting to hear back on it—in the meantime, we've already erected a shrine in her honor, and furthermore, we've sent her a running *ton* of bidness.

While it's relatively inexpensive and easy to get a divorce if nobody's got anything to fight over, that is hardly the case if there is stuff involved. You must pay your lawyer. You must pay your lawyer *on time*. Lawyers will not, nor should they, do any work on your behalf for free. You cannot fool them with "The check is in the mail." They *invented* "The check is in the mail." For a time, your lawyer may sit and listen in what appears to be a sympathetic manner to your manifold tales of woe regarding your future ex. But without a cleared check in the firm's account, those meetings will soon cease, and whenever you call, you'll be told he or she "is on the other line," presumably with a paying customer. Plus, you might also find it difficult to find any other lawyers willing to take your calls, and before you know it, you'll be marking your golden anniversary with that scumbag, like it or not. You cannot get out of this mess without a lawyer, so play nice and maybe your legal expenses will be covered in your settlement. But trust me, when you're free, you'll realize that whatever they charged you for it is a *bargain*, and you'll count it as some of the best money you ever spent.

Divorce Etiquette

You must not sleep with your lawyer—or *his*. At least not until your divorce is completed. Everybody *always* finds out and it never works in your favor. If you're gonna sleep with somebody in this deal, I'd say make it the judge.

You must not lie to your lawyer. It's very tempting, wanting, as we do, to put ourselves in the most sympathetic light, especially if the lawyer is cute. If you yourownself have committed one or more divorceable offenses, 'fess up—you do not want your lawyer getting surprised by your soon-to-be-ex's lawyer if you haven't been quite as invisible in your indiscretions as you previously believed.

You must not sleep with the person you are trying to divorce. This could have the unhappy effect of un-doing anything like grounds you may have had in this deal. The lawyers call it "condonation," meaning that while your soon-to-be-ex may in fact *be* a lying, cheating sackashit, if you go crawl in bed with him again during this conflagration, it's the legal equivalent of saying "Just the way I like 'em!" and the whole thing may get tossed. Now, if, on the other hand, *you* are the lying, cheating sackashit that's being sued here, then by all means make every *effort* to sleep with your soon-to-be-ex for the exact same reasons stated above. If at all possible, do it in a public place—you'll want as much documentation of the event as you can get.

In the case of double best friends between two divorcing couples, nobody in this group should date anybody else in this

group, unless everyone turns out to be homosexual. This means that if the wives are best friends with each other and likewise the husbands, one wife cannot go out with her friend's husband, and vice versa, during the divorcing period. Heterosexuals can't stand up to the inevitable comparisons, but if everybody is switching teams, this rule is moot.

Everybody needs to stay within his and her own friend group through this deal. Whichever ones you came into the marriage with, you ought to get to keep, and the same goes for the soon-to-be-ex. Any friends acquired during the marriage are pretty much up for grabs, but try not to be a complete hog. Pick out the best ones and tell them all the gory details of his many transgressions so that they will side with you. Let him garner whatever support he can for his lyin'-ass side of the story from whoever's left. Once again, if you happen to be the errant party in this deal, you'll need to come up with *something* to tell people if you want to come away with your friend pool intact. Feel free to use the Little Missy's mama-proof reason if necessary, because I guarantee *he's* told at least one person you're frigid. (But don't expect the booty complaint to carry much weight with the male demographic.)

Try to limit the number of people you whine to each day about your ex to no more than six. It's also a good idea to put a cap on the amount of time you allow yourself to expend in such whinage. Make a list of at least twenty other things you can and would like to discuss with the people in your life that have nothing to do with your ex, his family, his girlfriend, his

trashy friends, or the divorce. For every minute you spend whining, you must spend an equal or greater amount of time talking about those things. This, I might add, is excellent practice for Having a Life—which is the whole point of getting divorced in the first place. Your goal should be stringing together as many days as possible in which the name of your ex never crosses your *mind*, let alone your lips. If all your thoughts and conversation are still steeped in his essence, you might as well still be tied to the bastard. Move on! Please!

It's generally considered improper for the divorcing parties to date other people as long as they are still, in fact, legally married to someone else. A separation is actually supposed to be a time for each of the aggrieved parties to reasses their situation and try to make a clear-headed decision about the direction they would like to see their marriage take. It is *not* intended to be a "time-out" from the rigors of married life during which everybody is allowed to dally freely with various and sundry other hapless individuals with the utterly false perception that "it doesn't count." First of all, it "counts" a whole big lot to the various and sundry other hapless individuals who are being freely dallied with. I assure you that if you aren't personally doing any free dallying outside the home, but your estranged spouse is, it will damn sure "count" to you. One hundred percent of the time, the only one for whom the dallying will *not* "count" is the one doing the dallying. And he will look at you with wide-eyed feigned innocence and give you a mindless, "What? Why are you mad at *me*? We were broken up when I

moved in with her! That didn't count!" See? If you "break up," all that means is that you have to give back the CDs and the ID bracelet. That's not at all like the "putting asunder" required for a grown-up, real-life D-I-V-O-R-C-E.

Your kids didn't sign up for any of this. Make it as painless for them as possible. Unless your ex is a certified hound from hell, try really hard to be friendly with him if children are involved. He will always be their father and their children's grandfather, and it's too hard to maintain a wall over a lifetime. My friends JoG and JoAnne had what I believe to be the perfect divorce—for the sake of their sons. They maintained the family home and an apartment elsewhere in town, and the two of *them* took turns moving back and forth, staying six months at a time. The boys always lived in the house, and their lives remained as undisturbed as possible. The other parent was just a bike ride away. This is about the best example I've ever seen for divorcing parents putting their kids first.

It is *not* a good idea to perpetrate an act of violence upon your ex-to-be—or to arrange for someone else to carry it out. For a really close friend who's getting a divorce, you might be tempted to get a bunch of girls and go in together to hire somebody to beat the crap out of the louse. But you have to know that this is really risky. Yes, it's possible to get an acceptable asskicking done—and a highly satisfactory maiming and the ultimate out-and-out killin' as well—but it is *very* difficult to avoid having any of these things come back on you, no matter how much you pay the vendor. Along these same lines, I don't advise

that you hit him on the head with a shovel, rendering him dead as a boot, and then immediately "on a whim" turn up with a brand-new patio out back. Even if at first you're not sorry about doing this, you'll probably have second thoughts when they demolish your new patio looking for the body. Nor do you want to go out and buy yourself a chipper/shredder and feed him into it. The store will have a record of that sale, and off your happy ass will go to a place where there ain't no pedicures. The bottom line here is that it's rare that you find a man anywhere who's worth going to the penitentiary over.

I did read about this one woman, though—we'll call her Doris. Doris's best friend since kindergarten was Sylvia, and Sylvia was beaten to death by her abusive husband, Frank, who somehow managed to get acquitted, and that chapped ole Doris's hind end no end. So Doris made a plan. She waited a little while before she started drifting around where ole Frank liked to hang out and drink with his buddies. She didn't have to wait too terrible long on account of Frank was, after all, a complete scumbag, so it's not like he was *grievin'* or anything. Doris started giving ole Frank those sidelong glances underneath the eyelashes whenever he would look her way, and licking her lips and doing stupid shit that only women in porn movies do. Being not only a complete scumbag but a completely *stupid* complete scumbag, ole Frank fell for it like the chump he was and Doris just reeled his rank ass in—literally, for the kill. Yup, Doris enticed, lured, and otherwise seduced dumb, trashy ole Frank right into her boudoir, where, at a particularly vulnerable moment, she looked

him square in the eye and told him, "This here's for Sylvia," and she just stabbed him slap to death bigger'n Dallas. Called the police, told 'em to come haul him outta her house and take her to jail, her job was done. Now, that right there is what you call your *best* friend.

As good a story as it makes, we can't have y'all in jail for maiming and killing all the men who need it so bad. You're just gonna have to restrain yourselves and think about watermelon instead. That was Daddy's answer to any subject that was painful or unpleasant and couldn't really be dealt with satisfactorily at the time. "Let's just think about watermelon." Occasionally, if there was a heated discussion about to ensue, he'd suggest that we "just *talk* about watermelon." It did defuse any number of tense situations over the years, if for no other reason than the pure shock value of how stupid it sounded. I recommend it to you for those tense times.

Try very hard not to inflict damage upon the automobile of the one you're trying to get rid of. Do not beat his car into an unrecognizable heap with your stiletto. I know someone who did this, and the car was a Porsche or another one of those major dick-cars. She ended up having to buy him another one, but she allowed that it was absolutely 100 percent worth every penny for the look on his face as she flung herself wholeheartedly into demolishing his car before his very eyes with her bare hands— and one really high heel. Maybe we should modify this rule to say you shouldn't do this unless you can afford to replace the car. But if you can, go for it, sister, and call us to help. Just plain tire slashing is not nearly as satisfying, however, and rarely worth the effort.

Do not confide your personal problems to your prospective ex, and pay no attention to any of his own problems that he insists on sharing with you. One of our precious Wannabes, LizzieB, was in the throes of a particularly nasty separation from the man she had chosen to be her very first ex-husband. There was a great deal of vituperation on both sides of the fence, but he, naturally was the more deserving of it. Then one fine morning, LizzieB got a phone call at work from the prospective ex, all upsot and bothered, and he's laboring under the total delusion that LizzieB *cares* why he's all upsot and bothered. She does, in fact, not care at all. She's just glad he's miserable and feels no particular need to know the *why* of it, but he is determined to share it with her.

That very day, it seems, just a few short minutes before he called her, he had exited his favorite luncheonette/titty bar, having enjoyed a big ole greasy midday meal with a complimentary side order of pretty much nekkid titties that were likewise big, old, and kinda greasy. (His dining habits had contributed markedly to the demise of the affections of LizzieB, but you've already figured that out, I reckon.) So he was ambling to his beloved car, a late-model import that he'd somehow managed to keep just out of reach from the repo man, when what to his wondering eyes should appear but a big crackhead with a nine-millimeter! And the crackhead was needing him a *ride* bad along about then, and since he had that big ole gun and all the Gloom was packing was the pitiful remnants of his lunchtime boner (at its best, more on par with a BB gun), it's pretty easy to guess who got the car, huh?

And so now Gloomie's calling LizzieB, with a major whine going, alternating between pain and grief over the loss of the car—much more of both than he'd exhibited a few years back when their own *son* was missing for several hours—and the shock and terror of having had a loaded pistol held to his pointed little head while harsh demands and epithets, along with flecks of spittle, were hurled at him by the crackhead. LizzieB experienced a rush of emotions, naturally. She confessed later that her overriding feeling was one of relief that the car— unlike most of his other extravagant purchases—was not in her name. The bud of her relief was nipped, however, by her best friend, the semi-caustic and utterly cynical Dottie. After she and our Glide, LizzieB, shared a snicker at the misfortune of the Gloom, Dottie put the quietus on the schadenfreude. (Now, that right there is one of your very useful foreign words which means "enjoying the bad luck of others." My sister, Judy, and I can't ever remember it, so we took to calling it "Frusen Glädjé," that fancy fat-filled ice cream we were also inordinately fond of, though, sadly, it is no more and we feel no schadenfreude about that whatsoever.)

Anyway, so Dottie says to LizzieB, in her most ominous tone, "You know what this means, don't you?" Well, ah, no, LizzieB didn't think she did—other than that the Gloom was on foot and nearly got his head blown off. She couldn't come up with any shadow side to the whole thing. "What it means is the son of a bitch will *never* die. If he came that close and skated, you can forget it."

Try your dead-level best to be civil to the ex-in-waiting—*in public.* Your case will not be appreciably furthered by the sight of you hissing and/or spitting at him in public venues. Save those activities for when he shows up uninvited at your house. Try even harder to resist dousing him with anything—food, wine, or gasoline—especially in front of blabbermouth witnesses. Restraint will serve you well. But not too much restraint. For example, don't pretend you don't recognize him when a chance public meeting occurs. That tends to generate more tension, I've found.

Now, way on down the road, after it's all done and some time has passed, you might want to consider a stunt like a good friend of mine once pulled. (The man in this story wasn't her husband, but the principle still applies.) She was out at a big fund-raising affair when she spied a guy she'd dated for quite some time, who ultimately treated her very badly, and she dumped him. He considered himself quite the catch and flattered himself way too much in the bargain. She saw him across the room and also noticed when he spotted her and how he worked his way around the crowd to accidentally "run into" her. She played along, acting surprised and happy to see him—she was neither—and chatted merrily for a few minutes, then turned to a friend standing next to her. "Oh, Shelia, let me introduce you to . . . ahh, uhhh—oh, I'm so sorry," she said, turning to him, "what was your name again?"

4

Don't Be Skeered

I have met many women over the years who hesitated—for years after the term *hesitation* ceased to be applicable—to get a divorce, on account of they were scared—or as some Down Here say, "skeered" and often "skeert." One day there'll be a Berlitz language course in Southern—Y'allbonics, maybe—but for now I'll just try to explain things as we go. Some Southerners, of course, are completely capable of pronouncing words in their correct and original phonetic state. For them, the word would be "scared" with a long *a* sound. The same folks who'll profess to be

"skeert half to death" by something will also tell you that it was the "skay-ri-est thang that ever was," switching to that long *a* and giving it a few extra yards of length even. No one knows the why of any of this, but we do all understand it when it's spoken— and now perhaps you can, too. All the words mean the same thing, but you have to admit, *skeered* does sound scarier.

Anyway, the point is that women fear a lot of things when it comes to getting themselves together to get a divorce. Many women get skeered about money when they think about divorcing. I understand this. Let me tell you that someone *very close* to me (wink, wink) found herself married to a true compulsive spend-freak. And, as so often happens with these folks, his credit was crap—years of charging without the fuss and bother of repaying had seen to that. He always seemed to think that those pesky statements the credit-card companies insisted on sending out each month were mere suggestions or hints for payments rather than reminders of his legal obligation. And he took very personal offense at presumptuous calls from stiffed creditors. It didn't take too terribly long for the word to spread about him amongst lenders, and he found himself labeled "persona non credit" on pretty much a national basis. That only left *her* credit—which was so handily impeccable—for him to use and, of course, he conned (and browbeat) her into giving him permission and a card to go with it.

Several years and many, many thousands of dollars later, she decided she could no longer afford the questionable luxury of that marriage and began making inquiries into the fees of various

divorce attorneys. Besides paying her attorney, she knew she was going to be faced with having her income cut by more than half, and it was a pretty safe bet that, judging from her soon-to-be-ex's track record with honoring debts, she was more than likely gonna have the pleasure of choosing between filing personal bankruptcy or personally repaying all the bills he'd run up in her name. After selling several assets and paying off thousands of dollars' worth of crap he'd bought—for himself—over the years, the final tally of outstanding credit-card debt still stood at more than thirty thousand dollars. We never calculated what it would cost to repay all that based on minimum payments and 18 percent interest, but we were pretty sure she'd never live that long, anyway.

To say that this was a daunting prospect just woefully understates it. She was nauseous for months just thinking about it, but meanwhile, he was still finding ways to charge things in her name and she finally knew she had no choice and she sucked it up and did it. She divorced him and cut him off from her cards.

The first thing she noticed was that her credit-card balances stopped going *up* every month. The next thing she noticed was that, even without his income, she still managed to have money for herself and her daughter that she never had before. She figured up what the total of her minimum payments were each month and budgeted that amount as Sacred Funds—nothing could touch it. Then she started with the smallest bills and concentrated on getting them paid off completely. When one was paid off, she would add the amount of its previous minimum payment to paying off the balance of the next one. She never missed a payment on a single one and she paid it all back, every

single solitary dime, with not one penny's worth of help from the sonofabitch who created every bit of the debt.

She had to learn that *she* was ultimately responsible for her situation. Yes, he did all the charging, but he could not have done her one dime's worth of damage without her permission, and until she found balls enough to withdraw that permission, she was helping to rack up the balances. He had her convinced, on some level, that she could not survive him being unhappy— but somebody finally succeeded in pointing out to her how very easily *he* tolerated *her* unhappiness.

My point here is, yes, the price of freedom from this guy was exceedingly high, but the *cost*—financially, sure, but more importantly, spiritually and emotionally—of staying with him was far, far greater. The price of the lesson she learned about letting somebody browbeat you into violating your own standards in order to pacify them was a high one. We can only imagine what the ultimate cost would have been had she failed to finally learn her lesson. Pay the price and move on.

And see, that's where I think divorce is—or can be—a positive thing. I believe that we're brought together with the people we are for a reason. We bring out the very best in each other—and that's why we fall in love. Then, before long, we commence bringing out the very worst in each other so we can *learn* about ourselves.

I have learned—or at least I hope to God I've learned—that we are *not*, as I previously thought, put in each other's lives in order to observe and correct flaws in the other person (as clear and easy, not to mention fun and totally gratifying, as this

process would admittedly be). I mean, how hard is it to see in the case I just mentioned that all *he* needed to do was grow the fuck up and stop spending more money than the two of them could possibly hope to earn? Pretty danged simple if you ask me, but of course, nobody did—certainly not *him*.

Trust me, she did spend several years focusing on that aspect of the situation—trying, with absolutely *ze-ro* success, to get him to see the error and folly of his ways, and to change. All that happened was that he got surlier and the balances got bigger, in direct proportion to each other and to how much she nagged and whined. It reminds me of Aunt Mary's bird, which kept on pecking TammyCarol's little-girl fingers till they bled every time she poked them in the cage. TammyCarol spent much of her childhood standing at the birdcage, yowling, "Aunt Mary, your bird's biting me again!" She could not get that *stupid bird* to stop biting her, until one day, on a whim, she stopped putting her fingers in the cage and—miracle of miracles—the biting stopped!

For him to stop overspending was *his* lesson, and she could not learn that for him nor could she cause him to learn it. *Her* lesson, on the other hand, was to stop enabling him to overspend. And all it took was two little letters of the alphabet,— those being *N* and *O*—coupled with determination and resolve, creating a resounding NO! Why is it we can scare ourselves nearly slap to death about saying that little bitty word *no?*

Some women aren't so much worried about money and afraid of big stuff as they are the loss of the convenience and routine

they've become accustomed to in married life. A good friend of mine was in just such a situation. She had a great job, financial security of her own, tons of friends—an excellent life, except for her drinkin', cheatin' mean-ass husband. But, sweet thing, he did regularly take out the garbage, wash her car real good, and change all the burned-out lightbulbs. She actually stayed married a long time to this man, who was breaking her heart on a regular basis—and not being one bit sorry about it—just because she couldn't figure out how she was gonna get all those chores done herself. Now, this woman is not dumb. She's as smart as they come. But she couldn't see the illogic of her predicament. She was scared—scared of breaking out of normalcy and habit and tradition, and there's no question, their pull is powerful.

Finally, I jerked her up and said, "You can *pay* somebody minimum wage to do all that and more. And while we're talking about hired help here, let's just imagine that your housekeeper came to work drunk, lied to you all the time, cheated on her husband and used working at your house as a cover, stole from you, and was just plain mean to you besides. How long would you employ this person?

"Here's what we're really dealing with here," I explained. "You're married to a man who's a lousy husband but a halfway decent domestic flunky. And you're in a quandary about it? Hunny, I will come take out your garbage and change your lightbulbs. Be *done* with this guy." And so she was. Now she's got the shiniest, cleanest cars in town and household help begging to take out garbage. If you find yourself in a similar quandary, I'll

come take out *your* garbage, too. Quit investing your life in a relationship that's bringing you only minimal returns. Don't be skeert of going for more.

If you find yourself burdened with an overload of skay-ry things on your mind as you head down the road toward a divorce you know you need, maybe this next story will help you buck on up. It's the story of Dianne Mitchell of Shreveport, Louisiana— Queen Dianne, as I like to think of her. Queen Dianne is right up there with my ultimate hero of all time, Curtisene Lloyd, that brilliant, gutsy woman I wrote about in *The Sweet Potato Queens' Book of Love*, who, upon encountering a would-be rapist in her own home, literally took matters into her own hands. (If you haven't read about Curtisene, don't deprive yourself another minute; if you have, go back and read it now.) Thanks to my good friend and fellow scribe, the talented Bill Fitzhugh, I was able to read Queen Dianne's story, written by Francis McCabe and published in the June 15, 2005, edition of the *Shreveport Times*.

The headline read ARMED ROBBER GETS EXTREME MAKEOVER, and the lead line was "It was a beauty school knock-out." Oh my, was it ever! It seems this tall, skinny guy with a bandanna over his face and a big ole gun in his hand made the *very large* mistake of strolling into Blalock's Beauty College one day, slipping up behind Queen Dianne, the manager, and saying, "This is a hold-up." She thought it was some fool playing a stupid joke

until she saw the gun and he said, "Get down, big momma."
(Queen Dianne is, like myself, what I like to call a *normal-sized*
woman—not one of your malnourished-looking size twos.)

About twenty folks were at the school that day, most of
them women, and the robber just scared the crap out of them.
Some of them were on the floor crying, and he didn't take
kindly to that. He told one of the weepers, "You'll be the first to
go." This directive pretty much set *everybody* off, as we can only
imagine. But not Queen Dianne. She was looking for her chance.

After the robber got everybody's money, he herded one of
the few guys on the premises into the back room, and Queen
Dianne just knew there was gonna be a killing. But for some
unknown reason, the robber left the guy alone and suddenly
turned to run from the building. And that's when Queen
Dianne saw—and seized—her chance. She simply lifted her
not-unsubstantial leg and sent that robber flying. He hit the
floor and dropped his gun, and when he tried to get up, Queen
Dianne landed smack on top of him. Then she rallied the troops,
exhorting her coworkers to "get that sucker!" And get him they
did, with what could only be described as a vengeance.

"We moved some furniture after that!" Queen Dianne
allowed. Those women set upon their robber with clenched
fists, chairs, a table leg, and *curling irons.* Can't you just picture
it, and doesn't it make you positively gleeful? The article went
on to say that blood and urine flowed freely from the "victim"—
so much so that the students' white uniforms were stained.
They didn't seem to mind one bit.

At one point, he tried to crawl off, but they grabbed his legs and held him down until the cops arrived. Somehow he'd knocked down a beehive when he came in, so there was a swarm of pissed-off bees adding to the melee. He left "crying, bleeding, and under arrest," just the way we like our armed robbers. Queen Dianne was quoted as saying, "You can tell the world—don't mess with the women here! It's like we were saying in class, we have to stay together as a team. You can tell any prospective students, Blalock's Beauty College has got your back."

All I'm saying is, I know one place I'm gonna visit the next time I'm in Shreveport. I just want to kneel at this woman's feet and sing her praises and bask in her Queenly presence. And I know Curtisene is smiling down from heaven on Dianne Mitchell.

5

Who's Lying Now?

Let me just say, that whole "She's frigid" thing fries me. I hear guys saying that crap all the time. Once, me and the Cutest Boy in the World were just minding our own bidness in a local drinking establishment and this totally casual-acquaintance guy happened by and struck up a conversation. We exchanged the usual surface-level comments, one of which was, "Where's Sally?" That was the casual-acquaintance guy's wife. He launched into this whole deal about how, man, has *he* ever got it made. He's got all this swell free

time on account of ole Sally just *loooooves* to be busy, and so she was washing the cars and cutting the grass and cooking and cleaning and all manner of crap—for *him*—while he was out drinking with his worthless buddies. He ended the proclamation with, "Yeah, if she still liked sex, she'd be perfect!" And with that, he sauntered off, leaving the two of us sitting there agog. I mean, all we wanted to know was whether Sally was in the next room or what, and instead we got this whole litany of her activities, which did not any longer, according to him, include sex. Way too much information.

We talked about it betwixt ourselves for some time, the Cutest Boy in the World and I, and soon we fell to describing what all we *wished* we'd said to him in response. "Boy, that Sally—she's a nine-day wonder, doing all that stuff, ain't she?" I was wishing I'd said. "Now, *me*, I am one lazy-ass wife. I won't and don't do *nothin'* around the house. This man waits on me hand and foot, carries my ass around on a little pillow 24/7, but man alive, I'm telling you, I'll put out in a New York minute. So you tell me, which one a'y'all is the happier, you reckon?" The Cutest Boy in the World fell out of the booth, squirting beer out his nose. He swore he'd go drag the guy back in here if *I'd* swear I would actually say it to him. He finally accepted that it was just one of those things that sounds good after the fact and that I had no intention of saying it out loud to another soul besides him. Then he told me what he wished *he'd* said to the guy: "Don't kid yourself, man, she's just not interested in having sex with *you*." Frigid, my ass.

Now, I'll grant you that the sex drying up is one of the chief reasons divorces happen. It is one of those chicken/egg situations. Here's what I think happens. She marries him, thinking he'll change (and she's convinced that she can make it happen), but he doesn't. He marries her thinking she *won't* change, but she does. He won't do any of the stuff that she thought she could trick, force, or manipulate him into doing after the "I do's" settled in. So she gets pissed off and starts nagging and pretty soon he quits doing even the stuff he *had* been doing right, and she gets more pissed off and ceases to be in the mood for sex— with him—ever. And then he gets pissed off and does even *less*, if that can be said of a live person. The bottom line is: Ain't nobody in that house gettin' any, and ain't nobody happy about it. And lemme tell you what, if they ain't gettin' it at home, they gonna get it some-*where* from some-*body*. I ain't seen too many who will do without for too terribly long. And this is not a good thing for the marriage, although it keeps divorce attorneys' kids in good schools. So the saga continues. Enter the Other Woman.

Now, we can all see how it happens that the Other Woman gets into the picture. The mystery to me is this: Given such a situation, why is it that the women will blame each other? I have seen grown women physically *attack* other women with whom their piece-of-shit man has been indulging in all manner of outside-the-home fucking. Hear me on this now. It is not the *other woman's* fault that *your man* is a lying, cheating sackashit. He is what he is 'cause it's what he *wants* to be. I mean, think about it: When is the last time you were able to get a man to do

something he *didn't* want to do? Let me answer that for you—never. If he wants to cheat, he will find somebody to do it with, and he doesn't much care who. And by the same token, if he doesn't want to, no woman on earth could persuade him, by any means, to do it.

While you're being all indignant and outraged at this other woman, let me reiterate that your lying, cheating sackashit did not come to her singing your praises and telling what a happily married man he was, only to have *her* set her sights on him and decide right then and there that she was going to steal this prize away from you. Naw. What happened was, just like the casual acquaintance we talked to in the bar, he came around telling her a big tale of woe about how y'all haven't slept together since the last baby was born, and that was five years ago, and *that* child was just a drunken accident that somehow happened during the last "mercy fuck" he gave you before y'all were gonna file for divorce, and he's pretty sure, actually, that you're a lesbian and he's just been staying with you because he loooooves his children soooo much that he just can't hardly stand to be away from 'em for a single solitary second, except for, of course, this special happy hour he takes for himself every afternoon from four till nine, just to, you know, clear his head, before he goes home to you, his screaming bitchcuntwhorefromhellpossiblelesbian wife.

That's what he told her, and there is no telling how many other women he told that to before he got one to sit still for it. Trust me, if a guy wants Strange, he'll say anything, do anything, to get it, and he doesn't particularly care who he hurts in the

process—not you and certainly not the Strange. He cares only about himself and what himself wants at any given moment, and this is not what you'd call news.

If you are involved with this man, your problem is *not* another woman. (And if you somehow succeeded in running off that woman, there'll only be another one along soon.) Your problem is *him*.

And, more important, *you*. You are the one part of this equation that you can absolutely do something about—the only part, as a matter of fact. You need to examine what it is about you that makes you think you love and want to be with a man who clearly shares your low opinion of yourself. Perhaps *that's* what y'all have in common—you both think you don't deserve any better.

Sounds like you've got a bad case of Mad Wife Disease, where you've been living with his crazy-making behavior for so long, it doesn't even seem crazy to you anymore because you are completely insane. But you'll be relieved to know there *is* a cure. Mad Wife Disease is curable. Just step back and take the blinders off your own eyes and ask yourself: What really exists in this relationship that is making my life better? I forcefully emphasize the "really exists" because you cannot actually be in a relationship with someone else's *potential*. As in, "Well, if he would only quit drinking, everything would be fine," or "If only that other woman would leave him alone, he'd want me again," or "If he didn't spend more than we both make on racing tires and cashmere socks, I might be able to get my teeth capped."

None of that is ever gonna happen, but if it miraculously does, it won't be because you were silent and long-suffering. And tell me please, why would anybody aspire to be "long-suffering"? I'd say go for "short-suffering" any day. After all, it's *suffering* and I'm against the prolonging of it, whether it's mine or somebody else's. Well, that's not entirely true; there are *some* folks I could, gleefully, watch suffer for days on end. But I am absolutely 100 percent against the suffering of myself and those I care about, and I welcome any shortcuts toward ending it.

And while we're at it, let's talk about another mystifying piece of "logic." When Silly Girl, against her better judgment and the advice of all her friends and family, falls for and gets into a relationship with a man she *knows* from the get-go is involved with somebody else—or even married to 'em—how come she is invariably stunned and hurt to the core of her silly being when she discovers that he has cheated on *her*? And the wife or girlfriend is equally shocked, appalled, and dismayed that she *also* has been cheated on by this sorry ass. I mean, this has only been going on since penises were invented—how is it possible that anybody is still surprised by their behavior?

I'm a regular customer of Sharper Image, and I love to peruse their catalogs for gadgets I can no longer live without. They used to carry an intriguing item called the Truth Phone, which they claimed could detect lies emanating from your callers. The

phone was designed to somehow discern whether the person on the other end was issuing any whoppers, fibs, and little white lies, as well as any subtle prevarication, mendacity, and/or false-hood. It would light up a certain way in response to the truth and light up in other ways for various levels of untruth. Unfortunately, I procrastinated in ordering this invaluable tool, and when I tried to get my very own Truth Phone, it was no longer available. So now we have to improvise.

Let's just imagine that your best friend *has* a Truth Phone, and it really does work. You call her up and tell her everything that's been going wrong in your marriage, along with all your justifications for staying. How much of what you tell her is going to register as "truth" and how much of it will register as "lies"? Lies you are telling yourself that are keeping you stuck in your misery. It's bad enough to have someone else lie to you, but if you can't trust *yourself* to tell you The Truth, your situation is indeed dire. You can't deal with a situation if you won't even acknowledge what the situation really is. And that's no lie.

Hot Sex Fairy

Somebody once sent me a chain letter, with the requisite curse-threat if I dared to break the chain. I *hate* chain letters and all who send them. They make my skin crawl and my teeth itch. But mostly I despise them because I'm superstitious, and it is all I can do *not* to comply with the demands, regardless of how stupid I know the whole thing is.

This particular chain letter was from the "Hot Sex Fairy," and she declared a plethora of excellent justifications for having lots and lots of sex. She said it is a beauty treatment for us girls. The estrogen we produce during sex makes our hair shine and our skin smooth, and the sweat created cleanses our pores, not only making our skin glow but also reducing the chances of dermatitis, skin rashes, and unsightly blemishes.

She points out that sex is also an excellent calorie-burner after that romantic dinner. (Although I can't argue the calorie-burning benefits, I do take issue with the idea of after-dinner sex. I don't know about you, but I'm a pretty healthy eater and usually find my abdomen not at its most attractive right after a big feed—plus I am sleepy and not agreeable to being pestered, if you know what I mean.) But this is the Hot Sex Fairy's tale, so I'm letting her tell it. She said it's a very safe sport. (I'm of the opinion that sex is *really* safe only if you're having it by yourself. Once others are involved, the hazards unavoidably increase—but again, this is her tale.) She says sex is more fun than swimming twenty laps, and I would have to agree, although there *have* been exceptions. She says you don't need special shoes for it. (Guess the Hot Sex Fairy doesn't ever put on a pair of FMP's? Too bad for her. Could it be that Miss Hot Sex might need a little spicing up her own fairy self?)

The Hot Sex Fairy says that sex is an instant cure for mild depression on account of it releases endorphins into the bloodstream and produces a sense of euphoria and well-being. She says it's the safest tranquilizer in the world and is ten times

more effective than Valium. (I would argue that *good* sex produces those things for us, whereas *crummy* sex releases bile and vitriol and produces a strong desire to lacerate, if not decapitate, the person responsible.) It should be noted that in the male of our species there's no distinction between good sex and bad sex. This is because there is no such thing as bad sex for them. Men differentiate only between *sex* and *no sex*—the one automatically and universally translating as good and the latter as bad.

Having a lot of sex will cause you to be offered still more sex, the Hot Sex Fairy explains, because sexually active women put out pheromones, the subtle sex perfume that drives guys crazy. We can certainly all verify this, can we not? I mean, as soon as you have *got* a man, every man you see wants your ass. I'm inclined to believe this phenomenon has more to do with the peculiar guy-type behavior of just wanting whatever somebody else has got rather than any subtle sex perfume bullshit, but whatever.

According to the Hot Sex Fairy, sex will make your teeth last longer (the extra saliva produced by kissing causes less plaque buildup), your headaches go away (blood vessels in the brain dilate), and your nose won be stobbed ub no mo' on account of sex is a natural antihistamine.

Now, this was all right cheery information, and I didn't mind getting it one bit until I got to the bottom of the stupid letter (the original of which is in a basement room of someplace called the Dwight House Pub—no mention of where *that* is

and why it matters a damn. I was told that this had been sent to me for good luck in sex, and that it had been around the world *nine times* and *must* keep going. I had ninety-six hours (ninety-six hours!) to send it to at least ten other people or I would never have good sex again; I'd become celibate and my genitals would rot and fall off. This was *no joke*, I was assured. I should send it to people who, in my opinion, needed sex. (As opposed to the people I think *don't* need it—and who would they be?) The letter said I should not send money, as the fate of my genitals has no price. Can't really argue with that, I suppose, but I do wonder where the Hot Sex Fairy receives her mail and if anybody has ever actually offered her money in exchange for the guaranteed safety of their genitals and/or those of their loved ones, and if so, did she turn it down? The Hot Sex Fairy's gotta eat and pay rent, one imagines, and how can she afford to work for free?

I was further informed that the letter *must* tour the world once again and that I must send it and that this was true even if I was not superstitious. But, of course, we already established that I am. So *here*, Hot Sex Fairy—I have just sent your stupid-ass letter to the gabillions of people who'll read this book. Now leave me alone. Send me no more such letters. I don't need your good luck for sex. *I've* got the Cutest Boy in the World.

But hey, wait a minute, did you send me the Cutest Boy in the World for the last chain letter I grudgingly participated in? Wow! This stuff really *does* work! Quick, y'all! Send a copy of this book to ten people within ninety-six hours and get your

own Cutest Boy in the World. And if you break this chain, you will immediately be visited by the Redheaded Man Who Would Not Move! (See *The Sweet Potato Queens' Book of Love* for clarification of this curse.) Oh, yes, and then your genitals will rot and fall off.

6

Warts B Gone

A disproportionate supply of the world's woe is visited upon the Divorced Woman—"the De-vor-say." Not so with widows. I have girlfriends who have had husbands removed both ways—by an undertaker and by a judge—and on this they all agree: Death is *waaaay* better than divorce. Folks just can't seem to do enough for widows, who, even when circumstances suggest otherwise, are nearly always perceived sympathetically and deserving of much patting and solicitous care. Widows are fed round the clock by kindhearted cooks making home deliveries or, if they're feel-

ing up to getting out a little, by friends and relatives who pick them up and take them out for fine restaurant dining. Their houses are cleaned, their laundry is done, their grass is mowed, their errands are run, they receive flowers and lovely notes of condolence. Rest is foisted on them like Christmas fruitcake— "You *must* have some *more*."

We won't even *talk* about widowers, who are treated like full-blown total quadriplegics, barely capable of drawing their own breath into their own lungs unaided. Divorced men fare nearly as well. But a divorced woman and the woman trying to get divorced—they're just out there on their own. As far as I've been able to determine, it's not traditional in any culture to pitch in and help out these blighted individuals in their time of need. Let me hasten to remind one and all that these women did not start out in life with this blight. They *married* it later on, and it takes a while to rid oneself of it.

I found dealing with divorce to be kinda like worrying with this wart on my foot. I'd had it for a long time—didn't know what it was really, didn't like it much, but didn't think a whole lot about it until I started trying to get rid of it. Then that wart practically consumed my whole life. I just happened to go see a very fine dermatologist about an unrelated matter and thought to show her my toe. "Wart," she pronounced it to be. And that was a good thing to hear—compared to, say, cancer or some other major inconvenience. *But*, she said—I hate it when there's a *but*—and she allowed as how she was an internationally known and respected dermatologist, capable of

curing all manner of skin maladies, including many cancers, and furthermore, she could perform all manner of electrifying feats of plastic surgery—but warts? "Ehh, not so much." She said I had to get this over-the-counter stuff to put on my toe twice a day. Plus I had to use some stuff she prescribed that's actually made for *cancer* and soak my big toe and exfoliate it several times a day. And, I'll have you know, that wart is still hanging on.

I couldn't believe how difficult it was proving to be—in this enlightened age—to rid oneself of a pesky fungus. (I know you're in a pickle, too, trying to run off that pesky husband.) So, naturally, I turned to that fantastic tool of our enlightenment, Google, which directed me to heaps of illuminating information at a site called TexasEscapes.com. I think these are worth trying, whether to rid yourself of your own bodily wart or that wart-with-a-body you're trying to divorce. As you read these time-honored folk remedies, you'll know that, if you have an actual wart, you'll perform the action on yourself, but if, on the other hand, you're trying to save on attorney's fees, then wherever you see *wart*, you will substitute *your husband*. (Be sure and lemme know how these work on whatever wart you're troubled by.)

Mix equal parts brown soap and spit into a plaster. Put the plaster on the wart and wait twenty-four hours. After the plaster is removed, the wart and *its roots* should be gone! This one is so easy. It will be great if it actually works!

Make the wart bleed. (That's the good part if you happen to be using this as an alternative to divorce.) Put one drop of the blood on seven grains of corn and feed the corn to an old black hen. That's it. That's all it says. We can only assume the outcome will be a complete success.

Tie a human hair around the wart and leave it there for several days. Then remove the hair and put it in a nail hole in a green tree. Replace the nail, driving it into the hair so it will be stuck in the tree. When the hair rots, the wart will disappear. (If you're using this one, make no mistake: You nail the *hair* to the tree, not the wart.)

I don't have any confidence in this one at all. Put a drop of milkweed juice on the wart or rub a piece of wild turnip on it several times. Or you can try rubbing an old bone on the wart and throwing it over your shoulder. (Doesn't sound very entertaining, unless it means throwing the wart and not the bone over your shoulder.)

Gather the roots of pokeweed and fry them in hot grease. Apply the grease to the wart. After four or five applications, the wart should be gone. (I should think our human wart would take off after just one application if the grease was hot enough. If he's still around after that, turn the burner on high.)

This one needs some tweaking but sounds promising. Sit in a cemetery for three nights in a row. Then find a fresh grave and put some flowers on it while *wishing* that your wart will disappear. Two weeks later, they tell us, it will. (Somehow I think this one's gonna end up involving a lot more than wishing, and you might just end up in jail.)

As much as I wish these could magically work—on my wart and your husband—I think we all know we'll fare better with gen-u-wine dermatologists and lawyers. When we're wart/ "wart"-free, we'll know they were worth every penny.

My toe is blighted by this wart thing, much like many of our lives have been blighted by some wartlike spouses. But sooner or later, the assorted unguents and remedies will rid my toe of the wart just as you'll rid yourself of the one you inadvertently married and all the emotional wartiness that goes with it. And we will arise from our ashes, fair and strong once more. In the meantime, we could use some sympathy, some understanding, some refreshments, and a little fucking *help* around here.

I charge you, therefore, if you have a friend who is trying to get rid of a wart, whether it be one on her toe or in her bed, get your ass over there and help her out. And don't stop inviting her to stuff—that is just the worst. Neither kind of wart is contagious, and as someone who's had both kinds, I can tell you, dealing with warts is a lonely business. Think of helping your warted friend as storing up good karma on account of you might have a wart yourownself one day, and if you have been discriminat-

ing against those with warts, who are you gonna call, missy? Who you gon' call?

Women going through the upheaval of getting a divorce need all the support and help of friends they can get. By the time folks get around to actually filing for a divorce, they've usually been so miserable for so long, the actual divorce is just an act of mercy and liberation for not only the two people involved but for everybody who knows 'em. I think it would be lovely to have an announcement party to mark the filing of the divorce papers—happily divorced friends getting together and celebrating the occasion. There should be two parties, actually, one for the filing/de-engagement and another when she gets the papers pronouncing her legally free and unattached (see also Chapter 8, "The Divorce Party").

But you don't have to stop there. If your girlfriend is getting divorced, throw a lingerie shower for her. Hunnychile, she will definitely be needing new dritties—she can't be entertainin' no gen-a-men cawlas in them raggedy-ass drawers she's been wearin'. If you're de-gaged and about to be di-vorced and your friends have not stepped in to throw you a lingerie shower, you're just gonna have to get yourself new undies. But take heart, the self-employed amongst you may be able to write these off as a legitimate entertainment expense. Run it by your CPA, especially if he's cute. And now that I think of it, there should absolutely be a gift registry for divorcées. If your divorcing friend is the least bit bashful about registering for divorce presents, you might want to make a list of things you know she

needs and circulate it amongst your friend pool. Besides stuff you can give in a box, other excellent divorce gifts are baby-sitting, grass-cutting, house-cleaning, and the like. You don't have to do it yourself—give her a gift certificate from a professional. Casseroles and new men are also always welcome.

And wouldn't it be grand to see divorce announcements written up in the Society section of your local newspaper? It could actually be a whole stand-alone special publication, just like the magazine-like sections devoted to engagements and weddings. Think of the advertising dollars that are just sitting there, waiting to be scooped up by eager sales reps!

I can see ads for everybody in the makeover businesses—plastic surgeons, cosmetic dentists, personal trainers, hairstylists and colorists, nail technicians, and personal shoppers. Computer dating services would do well here, I imagine, as would churches with "Single Again" Sunday-school classes—talk about your meat markets! There is more action stirred up in those hallowed halls than any singles' bar in town, and it's twice as hot on account of you have to allow for the ever-popular "naughty" factor. And what about child-care facilities that provide after-hours sitters for divorced moms trying to plan an evening out for the night the ex is *supposed* to pick up the kids at five but is always somehow unavoidably detained? (Isn't that one of your more unbelievable coincidences?) I've noticed some of the oil-change establishments around here offer special rates for "ladies" on certain days of the week. I should think that any business, from oil change to yard-mowing, that offers a discount to single moms

would do well financially—and earn stars for their heavenly crowns at the same time. What a bonanza!

I'd love to read the divorce announcements stories. There's an out-of-state Society publication that I read monthly because they print wedding stories that often include personal tidbits about how the couple met or how the groom proposed, and of course, lots of descriptions of clothing and food—always of great interest to me personally. The stories very often end with mention of where the couple will be going on their honeymoon and where they will be living in real life, with what pets and the names of those pets. I love that part.

The *really* best stories are the ones that include "the funniest thing that happened at the wedding." Something like the bride and all the bridesmaids were posing for a picture with the flower girl and junior bridesmaids, and they were all leaning down at the same time to form a "frame" of faces around the little girls, and a good breeze got caught in their hoop skirts and every last skirt flew straight up over every last head and not a single pair of panties amongst 'em—it was all thongs and "commandos." Granted, it *is* hilarious, but it's more the kind of thing you would expect to be whispered and gossiped and tittered about in private, not see plastered all over the newspaper. Of course, I looove reading about other folks' embarrassments, having suffered so many of my own personal ones—makes me feel related to the victims.

Doesn't it just thrill you to imagine, then, the divorce announcement stories we'd be reading? Perhaps both parties

could each post their own announcement, with snazzy glamour photo, and include spectacular details of their own particular side of the story behind the divorce. Think of the newspapers *that* would sell. Follow-up columns would no doubt be necessary after each of the aggrieved participants read the other one's version. These would fall under the "Oh yeah? Well, listen to this shit!" heading and could go on indefinitely in most cases.

I'm thinking there should be two separate newspaper announcements—one when you file (the de-gagement) and one for the actual divorce. In the second one, you can report who ended up with what in the settlement, along with the names of the attorneys of any corespondents—might be helpful info to the readership, I'd imagine. Of course, as too many of us know, what gets awarded and what gets collected are often two very different things. Queen Janna's cute ex owed her more than 100K in back child support and she was thinking of holding a Deadbeat Dad Appreciation Rally—out in front of his country club—on New Year's Eve. It sounded to me like a novel and altogether lovely way to spend the holiday—I'm surprised I never thought of it myownself. (Our community has instituted a billboard campaign honoring our most illustrious deadbeat dads, with big giant mug-shot-type photos of the bastards and how much money they currently owe. Now, don't you just know the mamas of those guys are some kinda proud? Bless their hearts, I'm sure they did their best.)

I sure hope our Queen Janna had her Deadbeat Dad Appreciation Rally, and I hope she got photos of her ex's face

when he came reeling out of that country club after that big ole rockin' New Year's Eve party and saw all the placards with his sorry deadbeat ass name and picture on 'em. I hope they chased him around the parking lot, whacking him with the signs. This is just the thing for those follow-up stories. And we love articles with pictures.

Besides the opportunity for publication, there is just a *major* scrapbooking opportunity in all of this as well. After all, I imagine you'll want a special place to preserve and display all the little mementos of your divorce, like those newspaper pieces and the original photos from the private detective of your ex with whatever persons and/or farm animals he was discovered to be involved with during the course of your erstwhile marriage. It'd be nice to have it on the coffee table for the amusement of your guests, I should think.

My friend and SPQ Security Officer Emily has a treasured photograph of the face of her ex, standing on the side of the street like a commoner, as he caught the first glimpse of her, sashaying by in full SPQ Security regalia, looking very fine and very hot in black stiletto boots, black fishnet stockings, black *very* miniskirt, black Security T-shirt, red wig, and SPQ shades, carrying a bullwhip and looking like she knew how to use it. What a face on him! He looked like a little boy that a chicken got his bread. All in a nanosecond, you see stunned, pissed off, deprived, and unable to act quickly enough to rectify the situation, and

hup! It's gone now, chicken done swallered it! Now, that right there is a photo to keep not only in your scrapbook but emblazoned on your heart. You might think it difficult to prance for two or more miles in stilettos, but it seemed that day our Emily was born to it.

7

It's All in the Name

BooBooDonkey is a quaint euphemism concocted by one of our favorite grandmotherly, churchy types who simply cannot *bring* herself to actually use genuine cuss words—in spite of the fact that they were invented for a damn good reason—and BooBooDonkey is what she calls somebody easily recognizable by anybody else on the planet as a card-carrying *shit ass*.

Anyway, Queen Emily appropriated the term *BooBooDonkey* to identify the man she was separated from. And one day she happened to

peruse a few bank statements, finding therein a whole bunch of checks written by the BooBooDonkey to Victoria's Secret and another one to some strange woman for out-and-out cash. Now, she was already separated from the BBD, so this was just additional gasoline on an already substantial blaze. But just for shits and giggles, she asked him what the deal was, and do you know, that BooBooDonkey looked her square in the eye and said that all those checks to Vicky's were *gifts for his mother.* (Ewwww.) And he claimed he gave this strange woman the cash in exchange for Snoop Dogg tickets. *Snoop Dogg?* (Even bigger Ewwww.) Then, by way of defending himself, he said that he had never dated anybody else until he and Emily broke up. As it turned out, he got a pretty good education courtesy of our legal system on the *huge* difference between the adolescent act of "breaking up" and the grown-up world of di-vorce. Boy, what you wanna bet he'll never get those two confused again!

Now, while we're dealing with confusing terminology, let's get back to BooBooDonkey. Answer me this, please: If there's a hard-and-fast rule in the universe against calling a shit ass a shit ass, and if there's an all-powerful, all-knowing Being who is keeping track and taking down the names of who is calling whom by what names, do we think that all-knowing Being is too stupid to *get it* that Granny is thinking "shit ass" and meaning "shit ass" with every fiber of her being, but He doesn't "charge" her with it because she only actually said "BooBooDonkey"? Now, me, I think God is pret-ty smart, and I'm guessing He knows a shit ass when He sees one. And I believe He has about

as much use for one of 'em as I do—but that's just me. And, too, of course, if you're God and you encounter a shit ass, you can *smite* him as he so richly deserves. But if you're *not* God, then pretty much all you can do without racking up indictable offenses is to just *call* him a shit ass and move on down the road. Trust me, I believe it will give you a great deal more satisfaction to haul off and call him a shit ass than it will to call 'em a BooBooDonkey. But again, that's just me.

On the Sweet Potato Queen Message Board of Love, when the Queens discuss their men, they most often refer to them as BC or PITA. BC—Beloved Consort—is what we call them when we're praising them or are just generally pretty happy with them. At all other times, when we're whining about them and pitching a fit over something they've done (or not done), they are PITA—Pain in the Ass. I once took a survey on the message board asking about other pet names my Queens had for their men, and the Queens were only too tickled to chime in with the monikers they privately hang on their misters.

Besides the requisite Spud Stud, we had guys who are called Arm Candy, Booty Call, Cabana Boy (only behind his back), Catch of the Day (ditto), Chew Toy, and Flavor of the Week (only behind his back and after a few drinks). Other pet names mentioned were Follower (bound to stir up resentment sooner or later), Goobersmooch, Lordgod King of the Nummy (now, you just *know* he invented this one himself), Love Bucket, Love

of My Life (awwww), Love Puppy, Lucky Winner of the Dude Lottery (lest he think he's the only contender), Main Squeeze, Mr. Right Now, My Bitch (only said from a distance), My Boy-oh-Boy, My Everlovin', My Partner (too Roy Rogerish?), Person of Love (is this a job application?), Play Thing, Purse Hook (one of my personal faves), and the one the guys themselves love: Resident Hard-on.

One Queen told me that she and her husband have shared the same first-thing-in-the-morning greeting every day of their twenty-year marriage. She sticks out her tongue at him and he flips her the bird. They're not mad at each other, she said, just reestablishing daily that nothing has changed. I myownself have observed that none of 'em mind too much *what* you call 'em, so long as you call 'em to bed at the end of the day.

On the message board, we also discussed names for exes, which produced a shorter list. Shorter, perhaps, but it certainly packs a good punch as far as conveying the underlying feelings that inspired the new names. Queen Lynn discovered that during the course of her marriage to a real-estate magnate, he had turned the basement of one of his buildings into a home away from home where he conducted assignations with a smorgasboard of wives, not one of whom was his own. And furthermore, unbeknownst to any of those wives, he was also recording their antics from a goodly number of vantage points with very strategically placed video cameras. Oooo-WEEE! For what he ended up paying Queen Lynn in alimony—and all his "movie stars" to keep his pleasures out of the courts and the newspapers after

Queen Lynn reviewed and reported their performances for them—he could've bankrolled a full-length Hollywood feature film. He was dubbed Blockbuster thereafter.

When Queen Ann's son, Jason, was about six and his father, Richard, had already been asked to leave the home, some "other" kids took to teaching her youngster some "bad" words. You gotta watch those "other" kids every second, I swear; they'll corrupt your perfect ones in a heartbeat. Anyway, young Jason came in from the playground one day and asked Mama Ann, "What's a dick?" "Oh, hunny," she replied, "that's just a nickname for somebody named Richard." And Jason looked at her in all innocence and said, "So my dad's a dick?" Ann blissfully chewed on her tongue and hummed a happy little tune.

Included on the message board list, there was a Freeze-Dried Wackaloon, a Fruit Loop, a couple of Pukes, a whole bunch of Sperm Donors, as well as a fair sampling of Pecker-heads. We had several variations utilizing the ever-popular "Butt" prefix, including a "-head, a "-munch," and a "-plug," along with the quite evocative "-wipe-head." Many who're still painfully new to the divorce game can only manage a guttural and very heartfelt "*&!@^#*!" We know the proper wording will come to you in time. Perhaps some of the suggestions here will strike a chord.

Another entire category was devoted to names coined for the women the exes took up with—either during or after the marriage. One silly old man found himself befriending, as they so often do, a barely postpubescent girl, who convinced him that

his gray hair made him look too old. When he arrived to pick up his children for one of their infrequent "daddy days," his former wife noted a marked change in his appearance. No, he had not colored his hair—it was all gone. He was bald as an egg. When the former Mrs. Egg commented upon his striking new look, he laughed goofily and explained that young BritneyAshley-MandyCourtney—whatever her little name was—thought this made him look young and hot. More thankful by the second that she was no longer tied to this ninny, the ex-wife said nothing, just looked bemused. He mistook her faraway look for interest and proudly informed her that he no longer had any hair, any-where—he was clean as a whistle, tip to toe, stem to stern. Whereupon the new girlfriend was promptly and permanently named Shave My Balls Barbie.

8

The Divorce Party

You need a party! You have walked through the valley of the shadow of divorce and it is time for you to rejoin the living. You *deserve* a party. You also deserve a *medal* for surviving all this crap, but at the time of your divorce, a party will do you more good than a medal (unless it comes with a large sum of money attached). If you don't have friends who'll throw for a party for you, throw one for yourself, and consider inviting some new folks on account of clearly you need some new friends.

Okay, first things first: You've gotta have music at your party. We all know how much music there is for brides and weddings, but what is our divorce music? With the help of several Queens from the Message Board of Love, I've compiled an exhaustive list of most appropriate songs for the occasion—in alphabetical order, no less:

- "All My Exes Live in Texas"
- "Almost Over You"
- "Already Gone"
- "Another One Bites the Dust"
- "Beat It"
- "Better Things to Do"
- "Big Deal"
- "The Bitch Is Back"
- "Can't Touch This"
- "Celebration"
- "Cold-Hearted Snake"
- "Did I Shave My Legs for This?"

- "Ding-Dong the Prick Is Gone"
- "D-I-V-O-R-C-E" (This one was determined to be somewhat of a downer in its original form, being kinda pitiful-sounding and all, and not at *all* in keeping with the prevailing attitude of the Queens, so we went with our buddy Suzy Elkin's rewrite of it, which says, "Our D-I-V-O-R-C-E became final today/That A-S-S-H-O-L-E will be going a-way." Definite improvement on the perk factor, wouldn't you say?)
- "Don't Go Away Mad, Just Go Away"
- "Drinkin' My Baby Goodbye"
- "Fifty Ways to Leave Your Lover"
- "Find Another Fool"
- "Free"
- "Freebird"
- "Get Over It"
- "Goodbye Earl" (a sentimental favorite)
- "Goodbye to You"
- "Got to Get You Off My Mind"
- "Go Your Own Way"
- "Harden My Heart"
- "The Hardest Part of Breaking Up (Is Getting Back Your Stuff)"
- "He Had It Coming"
- "Here's a Quarter, Call Someone Who Cares" (Queen Kellion offered this amendment: "Take this ring and shove it, I ain't wearin' it no more. Here's a quarter, find someone besides your mama who cares!" Nice touch, I thought.)

- "Hit the Road Jack"
- "Holding My Own"
- "House of Pain"
- "How Do You Like Me Now?" (Our very own SPQ songstress Kacey Jones has an even better one, "How Do You Like These Babies Now?" all about getting a boob job after leaving the jerk.)
- "I Don't Wanna Hurt No More"
- "(I Hate) Everything About You"
- "I Hate Myself for Loving You"
- "I Love Myself Today"
- "I Never Loved You Anyway"
- "I Want a New Drug"
- "I Want to Live"
- "I Want to Be Wanted"
- "I Will Survive"
- "I'll Be Alright Without You"
- "I'm Coming Out"
- "I'm Free"
- "I'm Gonna Wash That Man Right Outta My Hair"
- "I'm Not Living Here"
- "I'm Still Standing"
- "Independence Day"
- "Is It Over Yet?"
- "It's Over"
- "It's Over Now"
- "It's Raining Men"

- "It's Too Late"
- "I've Got a New Attitude"
- "Jive Talkin' "
- "Jose Cuervo, You Are a Friend of Mine"
- "Keep Walkin' On"
- "Kiss My Ass"
- "Kiss This"
- "Left Me a Fool"
- "Leavin' Ground"
- "Lesson in Leavin' "
- "Let's Call the Whole Thing Off"
- "Liar"
- "Lies"
- "Life Goes On"
- "Little Liar"
- "Lonesome Loser"
- "Love Don't Live Here Anymore"
- "Love on the Rocks, No Ice"
- "Love Stinks"
- "Love's Been a Little Bit Hard on Me"
- "My Heart Will Go On" (Even though this one does crawl all over me personally and make me want to sink huge ships full of people.)
- "My Way"
- "Na Na Hey Hey (Kiss Him Good-bye)"—This is the one you know as "Na na na na na, na na na na! Hey! Hey! Hey! Good-bye" (A contender for best chorus)

- "Never Be Your Fool Again"
- "Never Goin' Back Again"
- "No More 'I Love You's' "
- "No More Tears"
- "No Trash in My Trailer"
- "Nobody Knows the Trouble I've Seen"
- "Off and Running"
- "On My Own"
- "Pack Ya Bags"
- "Party Time"
- "Real Man"
- "Release Me"
- "Respect" (Of course, I don't think one should make any major move in one's life without at least one Aretha song for accompaniment and encouragement.)
- "Sail On"
- "Separate Ways"
- "She Fucking Hates Me" (Such a sweet title.)
- "She Loves Me Not" (Duhhhh.)
- "She's Gone"
- "She's Single Again—Hold On to Your Men"
- "Sisters Are Doin' It for Themselves"
- "Someone Else's Trouble Now"
- "Starting Over"
- "Stayin' Alive"
- "Take This Job and Shove It"
- "Thank God and Greyhound He's Gone"
- "That's What My Heart Needs"

- "These Boots Are Made for Walking"
- "The Thrill Is Gone"
- "Time for Me to Fly"
- "Too Gone Too Long"
- "Watch Me"
- "What Part of No"
- "What's Love Got to Do with It?"
- "Who's Lonely Now?"
- "You Give Love a Bad Name"
- "You Got the Gold Mine, I Got the Shaft" (Our beloved Fifi rewrote this one slightly, improving it greatly: "I got the gold mine, you've got a little Shaft." See, small change, big improvement!)
- "You Suck"
- "Younger Men"
- "Your Cheating Heart"
- "You're No Good"
- "You're So Vain"

For me, just reading that list is an instant pick-me-up! Now, there are admittedly a few pretty glaring omissions there. But not to worry. I was just saving them for special recognition. For one, there's that Nilsson song that says, "You're breaking my heart and it's tearing me apart, so fuck you." Where is the heart so stony as to not be moved by those words? Or by such stirring lyrics as "If you were here right now, I'd rub your face in kitty litter, 'cause I hate your lousy-rotten-stinking *guts*, but I'm not bitter!"? That and so many other original songs by Kacey Jones,

our SPQ songstress. (All available on CD at www.sweetpotato-queens.com. What kind of Queen would tell you about them and not provide a convenient means of purchase?) Queen-O-Rama suggested the perfect divorce song title on the Message Board of Love—"Bite Me, You Loser Asshole." When we clamored for lyrics, PeachyQueen fired off some verses and continued adding stanzas all night long. The only tune she could come up with was "An Irish Lullaby"—you know, "Too ra loo ra loo ra, too ra loo ra li." Sing the title to that tune and see if you don't laugh for three days just like I did.

I think it's a good idea to pass out lyric sheets for your selected song list for the party. I do purely love a sing-along and this should prove to be a most rousing one. A karaoke setup would be excellent because I have yet to meet the Queen who does not love a microphone—or bullhorn, even. Melissa Manchester, Nancy Hasty, and Sharon Vaughn came to town to meet the SPQs prior to beginning work on a stage musical based on my books, and the very first person they wanted to meet, after Myself, of course, was the Bullhorn Girl from *The Book of Love*, and TammyCarol did not disappoint. She took them on a guided Blues tour of the Mississippi Delta, bullhorn in hand for making important announcements and demanding that assorted people come out with their hands up. It is mandatory when using a bullhorn that you demand that *somebody* come out with their hands up—indeed, making such demands is simply irresistible if you've got a bullhorn in your hand.

Seems a shame to have all that fine music blasting away without a central focal point to dance around. I find that just about any special occasion is rendered even more festive by a bonfire. Any good divorce party will have one. What to burn? Short of actual ex-husbands (the authorities take a dim view of this), we find that photographs of ex-husbands make some of the best kindling around. Toss in any clothing, books, tools, and/or furniture he may have left on the premises, and before you know it, you've got quite the merry little blaze crackling away—and that's the perfect time to toss in all your old "married underwear."

A nice touch for your party decorations is an enormous piñata in the shape of a rat. Even after it has been dealt the blow that sends its bellyful of treats cascading to the floor, the honoree and assembled guests should beat the piñata until it is an unrecognizable pile of shards. This activity will prove cathartic for any and all divorcées in the crowd, and may be revealing, as well. Note, for instance, the vigor with which some guests join in the fray, especially those who previously have been less than forthcoming about any marital discord in their own homes. Naturally, you'll provide plastic rats as party favors for your celebrants to pummel, throw, or stomp on at will in the privacy of their own homes.

My sister, Judy, threw a very fine party for her friend Clarice when she got divorced from her husband, Jackie, who was a preacher, if you please. Her man ran off—literally, ran *off*—in the dead of night with the Sunday-school superintendent, who

was, coincidentally, *also* a man. Yup, Preacher Man gave up "down-lowing" in favor of high-tailing—as in, out of state. This was ultimately really a big relief to Clarice. The *church*, however, is still in shock—but that's their problem. Clarice and Jackie were truly happy for the first time in decades.

(Now, I've got some preachin' to do myself on this subject. This whole "down-low" thing has got to stop. I don't care who you are, if you be gay, just *be gay* and get on with it. If you're pretending to be something you're not, you're just making everybody miserable, starting with yourself. Come out, be happy, and get on with your life, and let everybody else do the same. But you don't have to run off in the dead of night to do it and leave your former beloved to see the light the next morning.)

So, anyway, Judy had Clarice's coming-out party at Judy's own ex-husband's New Orleans bar, the F&M Patio Bar. It was a rare and beautiful evening. It was Clarice's coming out to reintroduce her to "society" as a young, beautiful, and re-available woman, and it was also a coming-out party for that ex-husband, Jackie, and his new partner, David. Everybody was okay with everything and happy for everybody else—this is New Orleans, remember. Clarice even hugged David and affectionately asked him if she should call him her new "wife-in-law" or "husband-in-law." David suggested he might be "the second husband once removed." This reminded me that my beloved mentor, the late, great Willie Morris, always referred to his wife JoAnne's ex-husband's mother as his "mother-in-law twice

removed." It restores my faith in humanity that not all divorces are bitter.

Judy's party was not only co-ed, it was also gay-friendly, so the crowd was a happy mix of straight guys and girls, and gay guys and girls—a little something for everybody. A good hostess always has a little something for everybody. Judy convinced her ex-husband, Jed, to provide free liquor and food for this little shindig, which he did on account of he never, ever really got over loving Judy, and he'd always do stuff like this for her. Never would *act* right, but he always was a big one for the nice gestures, which is not a bad thing in an ex-husband—a damn rare thing as well, I might add. It was just one big giant love fest with everybody getting all misty-eyed over how well it was working out for all concerned. So much so that Jed, who'd been just a wee bit overserved that particular evening, got all weepy over Judy and stood up and bellowed out a glowing toast to her wonderfulness, declaring her to be the Best Ex-Wife He Ever Had and vowing, in front of several hundred witnesses, to up her alimony by a pretty good amount. And Judy, she got all weepy over *that* and proclaimed *him* the Best Ex-Husband *Anybody* Ever Had, and she said that if he did, in fact, come across with that alimony increase, she might consider coming across with a little something else some dark and stormy night. Judy didn't go so far as to making him the Sweet Potato Queens' Promise (see *The Book of Love*) outright, but she gave a pretty strong implication of it. And, of course, he held up his end of the deal—and, of course, she didn't. At least

she never admitted to it, but I always had my suspicions about those two.

The dance floor—both on the leopard-print pool table and off—was crowded all night with perspiring revelers. By and by, someone—I think it may have been the ex-husband, ex-preacher Jackie—initiated the ole Dollar Dance with Clarice. This was so thoughtful of him, giving her, as it did, an opportunity to pick up some much-needed cash *and* make some new friends, both at the same time. Previously, I'd seen this done only at wedding receptions. But now, I ask you, what is the point of paying to dance with a woman who's pretty much guaranteed to be leaving with another guy at the end of the wedding party? Might as well spend your money where it can do you some good—on a *divorced* woman, for instance. And who needs the money more? I can pretty much promise you if you start plastering a sweaty divorcée with dollar bills on a dance floor, it's gonna pay dividends you never dreamed of.

Penises were a prominent theme at this event—as indeed they should be at any Divorce Party. They showed up all over the place, from decorations to food to party favors. As a Divorce Party element, the penis has a number of connotations. We're reminded, for example, that there is one less dick in the world for us to worry about now. We no longer have to worry about where it goes or with whom, and we don't care—as long as it's gone. We don't have to worry about what it wants or needs at generally inappropriate and inopportune moments, and that's a relief! We don't have to pretend for its sake that size does not

matter, and best of all, we're now free to express our interest in other ones.

I recommend lots of penis props for your party, too—meaning items made in the likeness of a penis, not things with which to prop up a penis. (Hopefully, we're through with having to try to do that anymore.) One can easily get penis candles, penis straws, penis lipstick cases, penis cigarette lighters, penis noses, and penis balloons (such a thrill to pop). For a bunch of women celebrating a divorce, I'd say the more, the meaner—this is the time to go full-tilt with any pent-up meanness anybody's been harboring. There's clearly no need for any silly, girly wedding-shower-type games at a Divorce Party. The bloom's been off this rose for quite some time now and we're happy just to drink and eat.

A penis cake is always a surefire hit with the ladies, opening the door and their mouths for all manner of friendly, light-hearted size, hacking, biting, and/or swallowing jokes. But no matter what its shape, make damn sure it's tasty, because it is a well-documented fact that as women, we just fucking love cake. One of my favorites is Italian Cream. Lots of folks down South have this cake for their weddings—on account of it is so *very* good—but we're nothing if not for equal rights and equal opportunity for all women, so let's just think of it as the Glide's cake.

Italian Cream Cake

An o-fficial cake-maker person can make this so it ends up looking all beautiful. I make 'em myself at home all the time and

they are ugly as mud fences, but they taste every bit as good as the pretty ones—and in the right hands, they are most conducive to being molded into interesting formations. I have no idea why it is called Italian Cream Cake—what's Italian about it? The good news is that you don't have to get divorced (or married) to have this cake, and it makes a ton, my favorite amount for cake:

Separate **5 eggs** and beat the whites to soft peaks. Cream together **1 stick of butter** and **½ cup shortening** and then add **2 cups of sugar** and beat it till it's smooth. Then add in the 5 egg yolks and beat that all up pretty good. Mix up **2 cups of cake flour, 1 teaspoon baking soda,** and **¼ teaspoon salt;** then gradually stir in **1 cup buttermilk** and add all that to the egg-yolk mixture. Then, into all that, stir **1 cup of chopped pecans** and a **small can of Angel Flake coconut.** Last of all, gently fold in the beaten egg whites. Bake this in three greased and floured cake pans at 325 degrees.

When they're done and cool, ice 'em with this: **1 8-ounce package of cream cheese, 1 stick butter, 1 box of confectioner's sugar,** and **1 teaspoon vanilla**—and you *know* when I make this or anything else calling for vanilla, I always use a running-over teaspoon. Smear this in between the layers, over the top, and down the sides, and sling a whole bunch of chopped pecans over it. Serves one perfectly but can be stretched to share if absolutely necessary—meaning, somebody caught you making it and won't go home.

More is better, I always say, so why not have a Gloom's cake, too. There are two good possibilities: a Ding Dong Cake or the Krispy Kreme Tower. A Ding Dong Cake, in name alone, seems fitting for this occasion in many ways. For your Ding Dong Cake, you can, of course, just pile up a bunch of Ding Dongs, but if you feel the need to pulverize a few Ding Dongs, this recipe might be more to your liking.

Ding Dong Cake

Mix up **1 large box of instant chocolate pudding mix,** according to the directions on the box. Then get **a box of Ding Dongs** (there are twelve to a box) and crumble up half of them and put in a serving dish. Put half the pudding on top, then make another layer of crumbled-up Ding Dongs, then add the rest of the pudding. Slather **1 9-ounce container of Cool Whip** over that. Then sprinkle over that the shavings of **1 regular Hershey bar** and about **a half-cup of chopped-up pecans** (well, just about any nuts will work.)

Krispy Kreme Tower

The thing that seems so just-right about having this as a Gloom's cake is that making a tower of Krispy Kremes just won't work. It falls down and it can't get up. Krispy Kremes are by their very nature unsuitable for tower-building, and I'm not speaking out of ignorance here. I haven't tried this at a Divorce

Party, but when we had TammyCynthia's fiftieth-birthday party nearly a year after her birthday, she wanted to serve, of course, Krystals hamburgers and Krispy Kremes. Our precious darlin' Wannabe, little larva queen Katie Dezember, teamed up with my very own Cutest Boy in the World husband, Kyle, to build a Krispy Kreme serving station. Katie had Kyle attach a bunch of spindles to a sheet of plywood so that they stood vertically, and then loaded them with Krispy Kremes. For a brief moment, the long rows of stacked sweetness looked lovely, but within seconds, the soft, squishy doughnuts began sinking down into one another, and by the time the guests arrived, they looked pretty pathetic. They *tasted* just as good, mind you, but the presentation was lacking.

In addition, the serving arrangement presented a problem for the shorter partygoers, like TammyCynthia. It was difficult for them to reach high enough to slide their own doughnuts off the spindles, and they were constantly calling upon us *normal-size* guests to assist them. This was not only a slight pain in the ass for us, being dragged off the dance floor to get doughnuts for the midgets, but being once again in the presence of the Krispy Kremes, squashed or not, we could not resist their allure and ended up eating far more than the recommended daily requirement. I'm certain that any number of other vastly inferior doughnuts would stack admirably, but then, you wouldn't have Krispy Kremes, would you? Might as well use dog biscuits in my opinion.

If you just feel you must play a silly game at your Divorce Party, try this amusing eating-based diversion. You know, of course, that fortune cookies are really not all that desirable as food unless you've been on a stupid diet and crave sugar in *whatever* paltry amount you can get. Most fortunes, too, have gotten lame these days, but adding "in bed" to the end of them just perks them—and you—right up. See if it doesn't. For example, "Your income will increase . . . in bed." Or "Beware of odors from unfamiliar sources . . . in bed." Back when we were "theme dating"—only dating guys named Bob, or Jewish guys, or doctors—TammyCarol and I would routinely add the theme guy of the week to our fortunes, as in "Pleasant surprises are in store for you . . . in bed with Jewish men." And "Your talents will be recognized and rewarded . . . in bed with Bob." Feel free to pursue your own theme at your divorce celebration. Copious quantities of wine and spirits enhance the entertainment quality of this game considerably.

Before the party activities come to a close, you'll want to present the newly divorced honoree with an O-fficial Sweet Potato Queen Jackass Certificate. This document states that, in our valued opinion, unequivocally and unanimously, the person just divorced by your friend is a complete and utter jackass, and we are all well rid of him or her. You can even get one for yourownself if need be, and at least you'll have the satisfaction of knowing that *we* are on your side. Having this certificate framed and hanging in a prominent location in your home and/or office will make you happy whether you're just divorced

or have been for years. (And it so happens you'll find this item at www.sweetpotatoqueens.com.)

For the big finale, Queen TammyPippa insists that everybody raise their glasses in salute and their voices in song for a rousing rendition of the "Hallelujah Chorus." Amen!

9

Delousing the Ring

Queen Susan, who lives and reigns in Austin, Texas—one of my very favorite cities in the U.S. of A. and home to Book People, one of my very favorite booksellers in all the *world*—wrote that she and her buddy were looking for some kind of ceremony that would "cleanse" the diamond from an engagement ring after a divorce. They figgered, and rightly so, that if anybody knew, it would be me, and they asked for my help. I could scarcely refuse them nor did I even consider such a possibility. I live, after all, to serve. Queen Susan was concerned about the possibility of residual ickiness having attached itself to her diamond after her divorce. I

wrote her back pronto to put her mind at ease. Susan, I told her, there is absolutely nothing to this diamond-cleansing process. The simple act of removing the wedding band from behind it has almost *magical* powers. Further curative powers can be obtained by placing the wedding band on a railroad track and thus fashioning a lovely (and *flat*) commemorative medal/lucky talisman to carry in one's pocket—to remind one of one's narrow escape from the fiery pits of hell or something like it. Actually, I recommend using a machine—there's one that will do the same thing as a train, without the danger and potential legal issues.

I find it can also be helpful to purchase (ideally, with funds obtained from the ex) an additional stone of the same size in order to have a pair of earrings made. Relocating the diamond in question to another part of your body other than your left hand can be beneficial, and having another—unsullied—stone creates a healthy balance.

Diamonds, as you know, are extremely hard stones and thus they are pretty much impervious to any bad juju emanating from guys, asshats or otherwise. It goes without saying, of course, that the *bigger* the diamond, the more impervious it is. As a matter of fact, when you get above the two- or three-carat mark, it is amazing just how very impervious they are. You could have gotten it from an ax murderer, and once he is gone out of your life, you'll find you can gaze admiringly at that big diamond for hours on end without a single thought of him muddying the experience for you.

If, however, you're in possession of a relatively small stone, it will probably be a good idea for you to go on and trade it in for one or two larger stones that will be more powerful. This will also help you to remember in the future that size really does matter.

As the anniversary date of your erstwhile marriage rolls around each year from now on, you'll be wanting to find interesting ways to *re*-mark the day—to remove the stigma from it. I like to think of this process as "palate cleansing," much like one would quickly take a bite of something wonderfully delicious to remove from one's mouth all traces of a rancid wine or rotten wiener. Imagine that, say, a *new man* is the something wonderfully delicious and, of course, that ex would be the rancid wine and/or rotten weenie. And don't forget, you'll have another—happier—anniversary to celebrate now as well—that would be the Day of the Divorce. I'm thinking this will be an annual call for jewelry and fancy new undies. The new undies are strictly to strew fetchingly about the floor during the "cleansing" on account of we Never Wear Panties to Parties!

When you were married, you no doubt experienced several occasions on which it would have been nice to receive a little "recognition," and by that I obviously mean "jewelry." But too often your various body parts, which were so deserving, willing, and ready to be adorned, remained devoid of diamonds. For any husband-types out there harboring secret desires to become

ex-husbands, you should know that failing to avail yourself of gift-giving opportunities is not the *only* path to take, but it can certainly give you some good momentum along the way.

For those husband-types reading this in hopes of *avoiding* becoming an ex, you should know that it's a rare occasion when *nothing* might actually serve you better than *something*, but it does happen, as you will quickly realize, should you actually give your wife any of the items suggested in list below. This is one of those "official" lists of what gift goes with each anniversary year. I don't know who compiled it, but I'm certain we'll come across his obituary one day and read that he was beaten to death with a shoe or several of them.

1st—PAPER. Right off the bat, it's clear the author of this list is out to get somebody kilt deader 'n a boot. You show up on your very first wedding anniversary with something made out of *paper,* and unless it's plane tickets to Tahiti, you are gonna get a major ass-waxin', bubba. The very idea, *paper.* Some poor woman has put up with your sorry ass for an *en*-tire year, and you show up with something from *Hallmark?* SPQ suggestion? Something diamond-studded would be nice.

2nd—COTTON. Clearly, whoever wrote this list is responsible for the alarming rise in the divorce rate in recent years. Hey, I'm from Mississippi—I loooove cotton—but I can't think of anything made out of it that would give me the

desired thrill on my anniversary. SPQ suggestion? How about *two* diamonds?

3rd—LEATHER. I swear to you, the list says "leather." And don't you just know he'll show up with some kind of leather *hot pants* or something, and then you'll have to kill him and then where will you be? He'll be pushing up daisies and you'll be in prison, with a pair of leather hot pants. SPQ solution? Well, once again, you just can't go wrong with diamonds.

4th—FRUIT. *Fruit!* The list says *"Fruit"*! I swear to God, for the fourth anniversary, it says he should give you *fruit*. I found another list that suggested *appliances!* WHO IS WRIT-ING THESE LISTS? I've known some guys stupid enough to give appliances (once), but I have not *ever* met the one dumb enough to spring for *fruit*. That's all it said, just "fruit"—no particular *kind* of fruit was suggested, nor was any clever way of *presentation* described. What? He's just supposed to hand you a banana and say, "Happy fourth anniversary, hunny—I got you this banana"? SPQ advice: You should buy *additional* diamonds just to make up for even *thinking* you could get away with the fruit thing.

5th—WOOD. He might as well just pick out a nice *pine box* to put himself in for the funeral. SPQ thoughts: something

gold or platinum—with a sprinkling of diamonds somewhere.

6th—CANDY. Okay, we've been married for *six* years and he's
given us a card, a cotton thong, a *leather* thong, a banana,
a stick, and now a Clark bar? SPQ sez—only your jew-
eler can help you now.

7th—WOOL. *Wool!* Wool is even worse than *cotton!* Guess this
is where the seven-year-itch thing started, huh? SPQ suggests that something sparkly should Save Your Ass.

8th—BRONZE. Which will be the color of our tan when we are
basking in the sun on the cruise we will take with our *girlfriends* when we leave your ass for giving us a gift made
of a metallic alloy. The SPQ list shows . . . guess what?

9th—WILLOW. Willow? What would a gift made of willow be?
I don't even know but I'm willing to bet you can't set *diamonds* in it, and therefore it is *wrong!*

10th—TIN. Okay, this list is just *sick.* They're suggesting *tin* for
the tenth and *steel* for the eleventh! I'm saying make it
steel wool and a handgun and let's just put an end to this.

The list just skipped years 16 through 19 altogether.
Seriously, it went to 15 and then it said "16–19" with not a hint

of a gift suggestion! It resumes with no. 20—like he's gonna *get* to twenty if he has ignored the last four years? I'm thinking his chances are not too good—how 'bout you?

According to *this* list, a girl's gotta put in *sixty years* before she gets another diamond out of the deal—assuming she got an engagement ring before she signed up for this tour of duty.

My friend Lori told me that one of her husbands was such a cheapskate, he berated her at length for "squandering" an entire *fifty cents* on a specially priced box of *croutons*—when bread was so cheap and she could have so easily made her own. She promptly adopted the Cheap Croutons as the standard of measure for all future purchases—of *his*. If he spent twenty-five dollars on CDs, she calculated she could have bought fifty boxes of croutons for what *he threw away* on those CDs. He bought a three-hundred-dollar suit? That could have put six hundred boxes of croutons on the table!

10

Catch and Release

There's been a national upswing in the number of men being beaten to death with shoes—by women—as you may have read (in one of my books, as a matter of fact). These shoe incidents are hardly what you'd call random attacks by strangers either, although with hormone supplements being yanked off the market and the gun-control laws, those kinds are bound to happen, too, sooner or later. But so far it's been men receiving what at least one woman thought he *really*

needed—a severe thrashing. So, in that time-honored feminine tradition, she simply made do with what she had on hand, and in her case, as in many others, that happened to be a fairly good-sized stiletto. I do so admire the continual resourcefulness of women.

Well, there's another trend on the rise—ball-snatching. I've told you about it before, where some majorly pissed-off woman (known as the Piss-ee) manages, through the sheer force of her own fury, to actually yank off one or more testicles of the man (widely known as the Piss-er). I myownself have trouble sometimes yanking the thing on the lawn mower hard enough to get it to crank, so ball-snatching appears to be beyond my personal capabilities, which seems to allow the Cutest Boy in the World to sleep better at night.

Now, I'm not sure if this is something an interested woman could actively cultivate an ability for or if it simply springs from the fire of a particularly annoying act on the part of the guy. I sincerely hope I never experience that level of pissed-off at the Cutest Boy in the World, and I'm quite certain he concurs in that hope. However, it is easy to see how it unfolds for some other folks, and we can certainly all empathize, can we not?

Imagine, if you will, the plight of poor ole Anita, a normally sweet-tempered Tennessee girl who discovers that her fiancé, Danny, is not the faithful, upstanding gentleman he portrayed himself to be but rather a lying, cheating sackashit. And when she confronts him with the irrefutable evidence of his most recent infidelity and informs him (hotly, we imagine) that he

should not expect to be marrying *her* if he continues these forays into the world of fucking outside the home, what does he do? He goes back to his house and *goes to sleep.* Uh-uh, hunny—do not be tryin' to *sleep* when Mama is still boilin' mad at yo' ass.

Toward the end of their marriage, a former husband of the very tiny Queen Teri tried that shit with her one night and she just sat right there, fuming, until he was far into REM sleep and she, tiny thing that she is, just tore all the covers off the bed, positioned her tiny self between him and the wall, planted her tiny little feet in the middle of his back, and shoved his very large lard ass right out of the bed. Then she grabbed the mattress and flung it across the room, whereupon he got up, remade the bed, and got *back in it.* So Queen Teri just waited and let him doze off again, then heaved him out again. This time he grabbed a blanket and wedged his big self onto the love seat at the foot of their bed and went to sleep yet *again.* Teeny-tiny Teri just dug in with her trusty tiny feet one more time and turned the entire love seat over, dumping him with a loud sound that sounded like a big ole ham splatting on the floor—which, I guess, come to think of it, it was.

After that, he went and slept on the cold, hard floor of the bathroom, behind a locked door. One thing about a floor, it's danged hard to fall or be pushed offa one—guess he finally figgered that out for hisownself. And Queen Teri crawled in that big ole king-sized bed and slept the sleep of the just, awaking to the peaceful knowledge that soon he would be gone for good.

He left forever two weeks later—he got custody of the bed, she got custody of her sanity—and did *not* have to serve any jail time, unlike our poor Anita.

Our poor Anita went over to the house of the sleeping Danny, and she apparently did not think of Teri's strategy for robbing him of a good night's sleep. Her approach was on a much more direct and personal level. Using one of her superlong acrylic nails, she handily—and by hand—removed one of his boys. We imagine that she stood over him, tossing it up and down in one hand, asking him if he was still so fucking sleepy *now*.

Some time after Teri divorced her own sleep-fighting man, she had an experience that gave her pause. She tried to move her bedroom furniture around and discovered it was far too heavy for her to budge. That spoke to her about the sheer magnitude of her own fury that night—and it made her glad she didn't have her own set of superlong acrylic nails. Having worked in a prison, she knows she wants to stay on this side of the bars. We can only assume her ex was similarly relieved to have escaped with his parts intact.

As it happened, though, Anita is serving only eighty-one days, and will be eligible for early release as soon as she completes her anger-management course. Though charges were brought by the state, as is required when there is evidence of domestic violence, Danny himself (who got everything sewn back on just fine) refused to cooperate with the state's prosecution, saying, "She's my heart, my soul, and my better half. I told

the district attorney I'm not prosecuting her." As a matter of fact, he planned to marry her as soon as she got out of the Big House. Who knows? Maybe they'll be happy forever now that they've established their parameters for conflict resolution. I know my own mama has told me my whole life that the key to a happy marriage is to never go to sleep mad. She just never told me what might happen if somebody tried to.

To prevent just such matters, many Queens around the world have abandoned the idea of marriage altogether and instituted a program of Catch and Release instead. This makes very good sense to me. I myownself just purely love to fish. I'll stand on a bank or pier all day long and just keep chunkin' it out there and reelin' it back, chunkin' it out there and reelin' it back.

Fishing reminds me of what I used to like about smoking—that it was something mindless to do with your hands. I always hated the taste of the cigarettes, really hated the constant cough and the stench in my hair and clothes. I actually hated nearly everything about them but the fooling with 'em—I just loved fooling with 'em constantly. Getting one out of the pack, tapping it on the pack (although, truthfully, I never knew *why* I was tapping it—I had just seen smokers do that all my life, so I accepted it as part of the ritual and performed it faithfully), then sticking it between my lips and lighting it for me. Taking that first nasty draw and exhaling it in one of the million different ways available to us, depending on what emotion I wanted to communicate at that moment. You can say a lot with a big ole lungful of smoke. I did love the exhale part—but the inhaling nearly killed me.

And then, the best part, using them as punctuation—the gesturing and the waving them around while you talk and then all that fiddling with the ashes, all the flipping and tapping. And I was always able to start and stop at will with them. I could stop on a dime anytime. I might smoke for a year and stop for ten, pick 'em up again for six months and put 'em down again, smoke a pack one late night at a bar and no more for a year. This was pretty maddening to my friends who were full-blown addicted to 'em, but it's nothing to my credit—just the way I happen to be wired, I guess.

What got me to finally put them down forevermore, despite my fondness for fooling with them, was when my old love Winston Brown died. (You'll have to go read *God Save the Sweet Potato Queens* for that story—it's too sad to retell here.) Anyway, Winston was only forty-eight when he died, and he'd been a heavy smoker since he was about fifteen, which is what gave him them heart attacks, I reckon. The morning I got the word that he had died, I went across the street to TammyCarol's house to weep and wail and smoke. I sat down in her courtyard and fired one up, and the moment I did, I swear to you, it started raining—on me. There was not a single drop of rain falling outside that courtyard. There was one cloud in the whole sky and it was raining in one spot and that was in that courtyard, on *me*. I knew that it was Winston telling me to cut it out or I'd be joining him too soon. I put that cigarette out and haven't touched one since and I won't.

Well, I won't say "never." If I live to be ninety, I'm definitely going to resume smoking again. As a matter of fact, if I live that

long, I'm gonna commence doing all manner of delightful things that I've given up because they might kill me. I'm gonna eat bacon three meals a day, every day, and snack on it between meals. Hell, I'll put butter on it if I feel like it. It will be nothing but risky bidness for me from then on out, I guarantee you. One can only be sensible for just *so long* in this life before it starts to wear on you. Ninety is my cutoff date for sensibility.

Anyway, as I was saying, fishing is like smoking for me. I love fooling with the lures (no live bait, thank you very much) and casting and reeling, and I purely *love* the catching part. Feeling that yank on the line and fighting the fish in to the bank and hauling him up to look at and admire, and if he's good-sized, I like to weigh him before I throw him back. I most always throw 'em back, no matter what size they are, on account of it's just so much trouble to keep 'em. Occasionally, if we're planning to have a big feed, the Cutest Boy in the World and I and our darlin' lake neighbors, Angie and Laura, will keep most everything of an eatable size for a few days and then Angie and the Cutest Boy will clean 'em and Angie will fry 'em and we'll just eat ourselves into a stupor. But mostly we just like the catching of 'em, then just giving 'em a kiss and letting 'em go.

We prefer to skip the bother of putting 'em in a cooler or a live-well or on a stringer till we're ready to clean 'em, because then you've got the *chore* of cleaning and fileting and putting 'em in the freezer until it's time to cook 'em. And then you've got all the cornmeal to mess with and the hot grease and blah blah blah—it's a big errand even if they are yummy. We just love

the standing around on the bank or in the boat, making idle chitchat, going through the mindless motions that make up fishing—for the sometimes-too-rare additional pleasure of the catching part. There *is* a reason, after all, it's called "fishing" and not "catching."

Relationships with men are a whole lot like fishing. It's highly entertaining to fix yourself up and prance around and see what bites, but you have to remember that, in the dating world, you are fishing with live bait and *you're it*. And in most all cases, you have to know you are just way better off with a Catch and Release plan.

We talked one day on www.messageboardoflove.com about some of the guys we've thrown back over the years, and how very glad we were for that. Sparklemama dodged an obsessive hypochondriac, and Softball Queen passed on the drunken psycho who talked a lot about how he could have killed his ex-wife and gotten away with it by blaming it on his Vietnam experiences.

SweetThing managed to forego a future with a psychotic ad exec who broke up with *her* because he'd inadvertently fallen in love with their downstairs neighbor, then several months later he called her back and said that he'd made a mistake, could not live without SweetThing, and had taken a bunch of pills—no doubt to prove his point. She prudently hung up on him, called the police, and let them drag his ass to the ER. Several more months passed and he called her yet again, this time to inform her that he could "no longer associate with her" (she'd been

blissfully unaware up to this point that they were still "involved" in his mind) because "she was part of his evil past." She cracked up laughing and told him she would be de-lighted to remain in his past until the end of time.

Then there was MsMudPi, who saved herself untold pain, money, heartache, and tears when she simply walked away from the mechanic after he cheated on her with a defrocked priest. She said that deal had Village People written all over it.

So the next time you lure yourself a Big Fish and he's right there flopping away on your hook, just remember that you can only keep him for a few days before he starts to smell, and there is only so much room in your freezer. So to speak.

11

Time for a Little Something

The those are my favorite words ever spoken by Winnie the Pooh, who said a whole *lot* of stuff that I like. In my kitchen, over the pantry door, I have a framed drawing of Pooh with his head stuck completely up in the hunny jar, with the caption "Time for a Little Something." I find that, no matter what the circumstances—happy, sad, mad, or glad— it's generally *always* time for at least a little something. With me and mine it's admittedly usually more of a *lotta* something, but I find most everybody can be persuaded to eat a little something, any time, all the time. The ones

who pretty much don't ever want even a little something—those are not my people and we soon part ways.

But this is the D-I-V-O-R-C-E section of this book, and no matter how you feel about the subject—happy, sad, mad, or glad—there's just nothing like a divorcement for working up a powerful appetite. All of these recipes serve one unless you are feeling in the mood to share. Remember, though, if you eat all this and purge (God forbid), you've got bulimia, but if you eat it, grin a lot, and eat some more, you'll get balloonia. Just so you know.

I've Felt Better but It Took Longer and Cost More

Stir up **2 cups sugar** with **2 cups flour.** In a saucepan, heat ½ **cup butter,** ½ **cup vegetable shortening, 3 tablespoons Hershey's cocoa** (in the brown box), and **1 cup Coca-Cola** (don't even talk to me about "diet"). Heat this until the fats are melted and pour it all into the sugar/flour mix. Add ½ **cup buttermilk, 1 teaspoon baking soda, 2 beaten eggs,** ¼ **teaspoon salt, 1 running-over teaspoon vanilla,** and **a cup or two of mini-marshmallows.** Pour all this into a greased 13 × 9 × 2-inch pan. The marshmallows will sorta float to the top—when they do, make sure they are evenly distributed over the top, not all wedged into one end of the pan and the other end just nekkid. You bake this at 350 degrees for around 45 minutes, depending on your oven. Keep an eye on it, and when you think it's getting

to be "time," just reach in with your pot holder and jiggle the pan slightly; if the top appears to be "set," it's done. What happens is the marshmallows melt, so you can still see the outlines of 'em on top of the cake at this point and you want 'em set but not scorched. You're gonna ice this cake while it's hot, with hot icing, so the only thing easier is if somebody else just makes it for you entirely.

A few minutes before the cake gets done, melt together **1 stick butter** (and you know I hate unsalted butter), **6 tablespoons Coca-Cola,** and $\frac{1}{4}$ **teaspoon salt.** Stir in **1 box powdered sugar** and add **1 running-over teaspoon vanilla.** Stir all this up and pour it, while it's hot, over the hot cake, right outta the oven. Me and my bestest friend, AliceAnn, have been known to eat an entire pan of this, still scalding hot, by dumping scoops of vanilla ice cream on it in order to cool it off enough to put it into our mouths. This is actually the recommended method of serving.

Don't Even Taste These if You Don't Plan to Eat Them All

Chewy cookies just slay me. I am powerless over a chewy cookie—and all ten thousand members of their family. Seriously, however many there are is how many I will eat—I cannot stop myself after the first one. The only hope I have is to never eat the first one. After that, they're goners—I am eatin' they asses *up* and that's all there is to it. These cookies are very

chewy, and on the rare occasions that I've made them and some-how passed out before I ate them all, I discovered that they *remain* chewy. I hate it when you make cookies and they start out chewy and then go all crispy on you, don't you? Well, these cookies will not betray you.

Mix together 1¼ **cups butter** and **2 cups sugar**. Add **2 eggs** and **2 running-over teaspoons vanilla**. Stir in **2 cups flour**, ¾ **cup Hershey's cocoa** (in the brown box), **1 teaspoon baking soda**, and ½ **teaspoon salt**. Bake on a cookie sheet at 350 degrees for 8 or 9 minutes. Don't worry—when you look at 'em in the oven, they'll be all puffy-looking, as if they're gonna end up being cakey, but when you take 'em out, they fall and get chewy and wonderful. People tell me they have successfully added nuts, peanut-butter chips, and all manner of other stuff to these, but I don't do it myownself. Give 'em to me straight and keep 'em comin'.

Jill Conner Browne-ies

That absolute *angel* of a Queen, Becky Coffey—also known as Choo-Choo Queen—brings me great wads of these caramel brownies whenever I get within two or three hundred miles of her, and I looooove her for it. She even changed the name of 'em in my honor.

Mix by hand **1¼ sticks melted butter, 2 cups dark brown sugar, 2 beaten eggs, 2 running-over teaspoons vanilla, 1 cup flour, 2 teaspoons baking power, and ¼ teaspoon salt**. How easy

is *that?* Bake it in a greased 13 × 9 × 2-inch pan at 350 degrees for around a half hour or a little less. Yield: one very large Browne-ie!

Better than Sex with That Ex Cake

You're already happy about never having sex with him again in this life, but I'm here to tell you, this cake is so fabulous, given the choice between it and sex with just about anybody else on the planet, you're more than likely gonna pick this cake—especially if you had, like, a sample of each.

Just mix-up **a regular ole German Chocolate cake mix** like it says to on the box and bake it in a 13 × 9 × 2-inch pan. Then the fun begins. When it's cool, punch holes in it with the handle of a wooden spoon—these are fair-sized holes—and then pour about ¾ **cup of hot fudge sauce** over it. After that's soaked in, pour ¾ **cup of caramel sauce** over it. Follow that with ¾ **cup sweetened condensed milk.** Chop up **3 big Heath Bars** and crumble them over the top of all that, then ice the whole thing with a bunch of **Extra Creamy Cool Whip,** sprinkle another **3 chopped-up Heath Bars** over the top of *that,* and then proceed with your vow of celibacy. You'll never look back, I promise you.

Rocky Mountain High

Claudia, Queen of the Rockies, took the already-perfect Oh, God! recipe (from *The Sweet Potato Queens' Book of Love* and

also *The Sweet Potato Queen's Big-Ass Cookbook and Financial Planner*) and fooled with it. Now, normally, I am categorically *against* fooling with any of these recipes because I think they have reached their peak in the evolutionary process just the way they are. I feel especially strongly about this regarding Chocolate Stuff, which is my favorite recipe of all time (it's in the *Book of Love* as well as *Big-Ass*). Don't e-mail me asking me for this or any other recipe—they are *in* the books. I have already writ 'em down for you once and I ain't doin' it again. Especially do not e-mail me asking me to tell you a recipe on account of you loaned your book to your aunt Clarabelle and you've just *got* to have whatever it is *tonight* for such and such an occasion. You should have bought your aunt Clarabelle her *own* copy if you're so wild about her—don't be asking *me* to delay *my* plastic surgery just so you don't have to spring for the cost of another book! My tits will be hanging to my knees if I'm depending on *you* for help, and now you want me to stop what I'm doing, which is always *very important*, to write down— *again, just for you*, you book-loaning so-and-so—a recipe? I am not thinking so.

Anyway, I have been *very* clear in my books regarding my feelings about Chocolate Stuff and the adulteration thereof, and yet folks persist in sending me variations on this theme. I have said it before, and I'll say it once more: I'll occasionally add pecans to it, but other than that, don't be messin' with it! I don't want caramel, peanut butter, raspberry, cinnamon, or any such stuff screwin' up my Chocolate Stuff! I sure as *hell* don't want

any fucking *mint* in my Chocolate Stuff! Don't even *tell* me you have done it. If you must do it, do it in the privacy of your own home and be quiet about it.

But anyway, Claudia modified Oh, God! and I have to say it sounds great. Not as a substitute for the original, mind you, but as an *auxiliary pie*, it is just dandy. If you happen to be a careful reader, you will catch an interesting aspect to this recipe where it appears in *Book of Love*. In that text, it's called a "chocolate caramel pie," and upon reading the ingredients, you will find no chocolate in it. This is what you call "a mistake." It should be described as a "*coconut* caramel pie."

So Claudia's modified Oh, God!—which we call Rocky Mountain High, in her honor—goes like this:

First, buy or make a couple **Oreo cookie pie crusts.** You can make 'em by mooshing up a bunch of Oreos (outsides only, no filling) and mixing them with **a stick of melted butter** and ½ **cup flour.** It'll save you some calories if you buy 'em ready-made on account of you *know* you're gonna eat at least half the bag if you make 'em yourself—but perhaps you're a tad underweight and this will help you.

And hey, speaking of, did you know that the Sweet Potato Queens have declared April 21 a worldwide Pie Kappa Yamma Day of Celebration and Feasting? That's the day the folks at the Centers for Disease Control and a whole bunch of other famous scientists from France and elsewhere declared that a few extra pounds actually *increase* longevity. Yep, those blessed folks—who we have already submitted for sainthood—have said that

the optimum state of being is *slightly overweight!* HA-A-A-A-LE-LU-JAH! HA-A-A-LE-LU-JAH! HALLELUJAH! HAL-LELUJAH! HALLE-E-LUJAH! Now, I don't know about y'all, but that is just about the best news I have ever heard in my life-time, and I will never forget hearing it for the first time. I actu-ally don't think that I am quite overweight *enough* to be *truly healthy*, and so I will be making my own Oreo crusts and taking full advantage of this opportunity to cram in a few thousand extra calories and fat grams in the process—before I ever take the first bite of the pie. That's how you get in shape, after all, just one little bit at a time over time. Slow and steady wins the race and all that.

Okay, so *next*, melt ½ **stick of butter** and add ½ **cup finely chopped almonds** to it and then put 'em on the Oreo crust and kinda pat 'em down into it a little bit and bake it at 350 degrees for about 10 minutes—just wanna turn the almonds golden brown is all.

Then mix together 8 **ounces of softened cream cheese, 16 ounces of Cool Whip** and **1 14-ounce can of sweetened con-densed milk** and pour all that into the pie shells. Then mix **7 ounces of coconut flakes** with **1 cup of almonds** and ½ **stick melted butter.** Spread it all on a cookie sheet and toast it in the oven, stirring a lot to make sure it just gets brown and not burned. Spread the toasty mixture over the two pies.

Finally, take a **12-ounce jar of caramel sauce** and warm it a little by putting the jar in a bowl of hot water for a few minutes (this way it pours easier). Pour half of it over each of the pies

and then hire somebody to come over and pry your hands off of 'em and take 'em away from you just long enough to put 'em in the freezer for a little while so they firm up a little bit. I'd say two pies, two folks, two spoons—and that other person should be a *very* close friend.

Fatten-You-Right-Up Rolls

Queen Sherry gave me another variation on a theme that I find totally acceptable—just to show how very flexible I can be. Sherry said that if you're in the mood for some of the Fatten-You-Right-Up Rolls, from *Big-Ass*, you might like to double all the ingredients, which would mean using **2 sticks melted butter, 2 cups sour cream,** and **2 heaping cups self-rising flour,** and then add **1 pound of grated sharp Cheddar** to it all. She says to bake 'em in a big muffin pan at 400 degrees until they turn the shade of brown that you like. Yum . . . warm, fluffy *cheesy* globs of fat—and, of course, you can *always* butter 'em before you eat 'em if you're still a little too thin to be really healthy.

Variations are fine, quite often, but somebody sent me a clipping of an article local newspaper featuring a chef touting his *bacon* ice cream. I'm sorry—this is a desecration of two sacred food items in my opinion, and I am not amused.

And now, without even trying, we've moved out of the *sweet* food arena and into the cheesy/salty group. It's all equally important, of course.

The Holy Mound

Ali, woman of steel, is famous for her cheesy creation known as the Holy Mound and you will be tempted to worship at the altar thereof—for its ease as well as its cheese. Just take **a can of "whomp" crescent rolls.** (You "whomp" the can on the edge of the cabinet to open 'em.) Unroll 'em, separating them into two 4-sheet rectangles. Fry up **a big wad of bacon,** allowing, of course, for the massive amounts you will want/need to consume during the construction of this dish, and crumble up as much of it as you can stand to *not* eat on the spot and put it on one of the rectangles of dough. Put **a big wad of smoked cheese**—Gouda would be good—on top of the bacon. A half pound is a good amount of cheese, and you can cut it up in little hunks or strips if you want to but you don't have to. Cover the cheese with **a good handful of dark brown sugar** and put another **good handful of chopped pecans** on top of that. Cover all of that with the other rectangle of dough and pinch the edges of the dough together to make a little package. Bake it at around 375 degrees or whatever your can of whomp dough calls for normally—just until it turns brown and the top seems tappable. This'll take a tad longer than it does to just bake the normal crescent rolls. You can cut it into wedges or just let people hack away at it at will—just don't get in their way. If you've got an iron will, you *could* make this up a couple days ahead of when you plan to serve it and keep it covered with plastic in the refrigerator, taking it out to bake right before your guests arrive—but I could never do that.

Artichoke Nibbles

Well, that's what our Katie Dezember, aka Katie Christmas, calls
'em. Artichoke *Gobbles* would be more accurate. Katie, from
Bakersfield, California, is widely believed to be the World's
Most Perfect Person, and I am telling you, it is The Truth. She
comes to visit us several times a year, including for at least a
month in the summer, and we have not *yet* been ready for her
to go. Last summer she joined us—the Cutest Boy in the World,
Bo-Peep, her buddy Olivia, Mom and Dad Jennings, and me—
on a weeklong cruise and then stayed with us, in our house, for
a month, and we *still* didn't want her to leave. Tell me another
houseguest—or anyone—you've ever heard that said about.
Our lives will not be complete or anywhere near satisfactory
until we can pry her away from that family of hers in
Bakersfield—who selfishly try to keep her all to themselves—
and get her permanently relocated *here*, where *we* can have her
all to ourselves. Anyway, Katie got this recipe from one of her
sisters, Cheri or Becky, I don't care which one, they're *both* guilty
of trying to keep her in California. Those sisters claim it makes
something like seventy-five, which is mystifying to me because
when Katie and I make it, it only makes two.

You drain the juice from **1 6-ounce jar of artichoke hearts**
into a frying pan, then drain **a second one** into the garbage.
Chop all the artichokes and set 'em aside. Chop up **a small
onion** and **a garlic clove** and sauté 'em in the artichoke juice for
about 5 minutes. In a bowl, beat **4 eggs** and add in ¼ **cup bread**

crumbs, ¼ teaspoon salt, ¼ teaspoon black or red pepper, ⅛ teaspoon oregano, and ⅛ teaspoon chili powder. Stir in **2 cups grated sharp Cheddar, 2 tablespoons chopped parsley,** and the **chopped artichokes.** Bake it in an 11-inch baking pan at 325 degrees for about 30 minutes. You can cut it into squares when it's cool and you can prolly eat them all yourownself.

One More Reason to Eat Fritos

Queen Penny knows all too well that we are constantly looking for new and improved foodstuffs that can be consumed via Fritos because it is important to our health and well-being to eat as many Fritos as we possibly can in our lifetimes. It should be noted, however, that this dish is prolly good on dirt-clods, being just your perfect, all-purpose green stuff.

Get **4 ripe avocados.** Queen Penny wants to be sure that everybody knows you gotta peel 'em and remove that *seed* before you can use 'em. Okay, got it. Next, put the peeled, de-seeded avocados in a food processor along with **16 ounces of sour cream, 3 ounces cream cheese, 1 small can diced green chilis, 1 10-ounce can Rotel tomatoes, 2 teaspoons salt, 1 tablespoon garlic powder,** and **1 teaspoon lemon juice.** Whirl it around in there a few times to blend it all together, then remove the blades so you don't cut yourself when you scoop it out and eat it with your bare hands.

We do not expect that our Pie Kappa Yamma Day of Celebration and Feasting will be a *dry* celebration, and we naturally insist that you and your guests enjoy liberal quantities of our own special celebratory libations, the Panty Remover Margaritas as well as the Ruby Red ReVirginators. These mixes are available for next to nothing in the store at www.sweetpotato-queens.com, and do remember that your purchase of these and other SPQ products will enable this aging Queen to receive all manner of rejuvenating operations, and we thank you very much for your support.

Queen Mimi Jane, of the Luscious Queens of North Carolina, offers us her recipe for yet another Queenly libation:

Slushy, Lushy Lemonade

Start with **a fifth of Southern Comfort** (you decide if it's an 80- or a 100-proof occasion) and mix in **6 ounces frozen lemonade concentrate** and **6 ounces frozen orange juice concentrate.** (These amounts could be doubled if you need to dilute the alcohol a bit for a particular crowd—you know who *they* are.) Add **2 liters of citrus soda**—I would personally prefer **7-Up,** but **Mountain Dew** could stand in for all or half, if you wanted a boatload of caffeine thrown in for good measure. If for some reason you need to *camouflage* this drink, say, for example, so the other Baptists at the picnic don't whine for some of it, you can pour it into the empty two-liter bottles or smaller individual plastic drink bottles, and nobody will ever suspect a thing! I call

that clever. Put the bottles in the freezer until they reach the desired slush consistency and then just lap 'em up.

Now, if you've read the rest of my books (and I certainly hope you have) and if you've been to www.sweetpotatoqueens.com (and I certainly hope you have) and if you've joined the Message Board of Love (and I certainly hope you have) then you absolutely know who Jay is. Jay, also known to members of the Message Board of Love as Cupcake, is the one who makes our website work. (Jay Sones is the person who is responsible for *anything* that works—I am usually the person responsible for all the stuff that doesn't.) We used to call Jay our captive computer nerd because we had managed to hem him up in our office and we kept him chained to his desk, awaiting our latest whims, 24/7, but somehow he escaped and went to New York City— an excellent place to hide out, by the way. He still keeps us going, but he's not nearly so available to us anymore on account of my esteemed publisher, Random House, *hired* him, which took a great deal of unmitigated gall, but they seem real pleased with themselves about it all. Random House is not the only drain on Jay's time—there's also this *Katy* person we have to contend and compete with and she is forevermore wanting *something*, I swear. But, consorting with the lovely Miss Tackett has greatly improved Jay's disposition and so we tolerate her pretty well. (Cupcake is not such a misnomer anymore. Pre-Katy, he was really more of a Crabcake, truth be told.) Plus, we

had dinner with them one night in New York and I found out that she *eats her fat*—which, of course, totally endeared her to me, and I was thrilled to find her to be such a kindred spirit.

So, naturally, I had to have some Katy Tackett specialties in here. She did not disappoint.

Raccoon Loaf

Katy actually calls this one Flame Loaf, but one time when she and Jay were taking it to a party in New York, they found a piece of paper with a photo of a raccoon and the caption reading, "Raccoon—13 pounds." The Flame Loaf was all wrapped up in foil and so they taped the "Raccoon—13 pounds" thing to the outside of the package and just handed it to the hostess upon arrival, with no word of explanation. Everybody there knew Jay and Katy were from Mississippi, so they were only too ready to believe they were eating a varmint.

Brown **1 chub of hot pork sausage** with **1 small chopped onion**. Drain the bucket of grease off and set the mixture aside. On an ungreased cookie sheet, spread out **2 "whomp" pizza crusts** (the ones in a can that you "whomp" on the edge of the cabinet to open—just like the biscuits, only pizza dough) and put a fair amount of **Monterey Jack cheese** all over 'em and then put half the sausage mixture on each one and top with as many **jalapeño slices** as you like. Now you want to kinda roll 'em up like calzones—just grab one side and fold and/or roll it up to the other side as best you can and then do the same with the other

one, pinching the edges together as you go to keep the goo from coming out. You can make one really hot and spicy for yourself and one kinda wimpy for other folks if you like. You bake 'em at 350 degrees for about 10 minutes, just long enough for the crusts to get golden. These are good hot, cold, room temperature, whatever, and you can freeze 'em for future use if you need to. Just let folks hack off as much as they want and eat it however they want to. Many folks think it's only proper to eat raccoon with a fork, but who cares what they think?

Christmas Salad

I think this one may actually have been Jay's recipe. It seems more in keeping with his level of culinary skill. It's called Christmas Salad on account of it's red and green, don't you know.

Into a very large bowl, dump **1 big bag of Golden Flake Hot Chips** and **1 big bag of Golden Flake Pickle Chips.** Toss lightly. Ta-da!

Now, I've seen lots of couples come and go, wax and wane, ebb and flow over my lifetime, and when you get to know folks, it's usually no mystery why.

My dear friends Angie and Laura have been together for fourteen years and they've been *happy*, which I think is the most important thing here. I do know plenty of couples who've been

together longer, but they've hated—or at best tolerated—each other's guts for years. I see nothing commendable about *enduring* life together, but that's just me. Anyway, Angie and Laura are as happy as they can be and it's great to be around 'em. It is *especially* great to be around 'em when Angie has made her banana pudding. This is *the* best banana pudding I have ever had in my life, and I have pretty much made an avocation out of going around and trying banana puddings whenever and wherever I get the chance. If I could find some folks who would pay me to do this, I'd take it up full-time. So trust me when I tell you this is some *fine* banana pudding. I think it may be a key element in the enduring happiness in the home of Angie and Laura. Indeed, if there was anything that could induce me to "switch teams," as it were, this Nanner Puddin' might be the pivot point.

Who Needs Him? Nanner Puddin'

This is so fabulous because it requires zero cooking, and if you're of a mind to (and I hope you're not, but anyway if you are), you can substitute low-fat or no-fat everything in here, and unless you've got another full-fat bowl of it right there beside it, you'll never taste the difference.

Mix up **1 large package of instant banana pudding** with ⅓ **cup liquid Coffee-Mate** (I personally *adore* Coffee-Mate and like to make my coffee more of a milkshake with the stuff— coffee purists are appalled, but try to imagine how little I care) and **2½ cups cold milk.** Then add (yum) **1 can Eagle Brand**

sweetened condensed milk (y'all *know* how I feel about this stuff—it's all I can do to not eat it all right out of the can!) and **1 12-ounce tub of Extra Creamy Cool Whip.** Line a pan or bowl with miniature **vanilla wafers** and **the mandatory sliced bananas (prolly around 3 will do it),** and then just alternate layers of wafers, bananas, and goo until you run out of goo. Now, me, I love the vanilla wafers and goo more than anything—I like for the bananas to be in there for the flavor and all, but what I reeeeally want is lotsa vanilla wafers and goo. I don't think it is possible to have too many vanilla wafers in this—I'm sure you agree.

Fuzzy Navel Cake

Just a little more sweet stuff! Lee Einhaus—Southern Belle on the Message Board of Love—gave us this recipe for Fuzzy Navel Cake. It looks purty enough for a weddin' shower, and it's not only sweet, but full of al-kee-hall as well—so perfect! It's a bigger pain in the ass than I'm generally willing to put up with in a recipe, but prolly you could get somebody to make it for you. I myself would be getting *Lee* to make it since *she* brought it up.

Okay, to get started, you heat the oven to 350. Then grease and flour a 12-cup Bundt pan. Sprinkle ½ **cup dark brown sugar** evenly in the bottom of the pan and then arrange **peach slices (1 29-ounce can, well-drained)** on top of that. Then put a **maraschino cherry** in between the peach slices.

Next, get a big bowl and combine **1 "plus yellow" cake mix,**

It's kinda like bankruptcy. Okay, not kinda, it's a *lot* like bankruptcy. The fact that you're completely buried under mountains of debt that you can never hope to repay is a tragedy. That there exists an avenue of relief is a wonderful thing. Nobody ever *wants* to get a divorce—or be forced into bankruptcy—but for anybody who's ever been faced with what appear to be insurmountable obstacles and known the feelings of panic and terror and helplessness, and then miraculously been handed their freedom, well, it changes your perspective and it certainly curbs your desire to judge others in this regard. Nothing like walkin' in them shoes for a mile or two.

I don't know what your situation is that's bringing you to the brink of divorce, but I do know a lot of what you're going through and I want to share with you a few thoughts that were shared with me in my bad times, thoughts that helped me. I hope they will help you, too.

Your reasons for wanting a divorce don't have to be anybody else's reasons.

Just because you have been taught something all your life doesn't necessarily mean it was good teaching. And, by the same token, just because it's different, like "Nobody else in my family's ever been divorced," doesn't mean it's *bad*. Just because something makes you uncomfortable doesn't mean it is a bad thing—it might just mean that it's outside what you were taught all your life, which, as we just said, isn't necessarily a good thing.

There are two sides to *many* things, and if your situation is one of those dual-sided deals, I hope you'll look at *your* side, as in where *you* were wrong, and try earnestly to learn from your mistakes.

Contrary to popular belief, there are *not* two sides to everything. *There are not two sides to abuse.* Many people will listen to your side and talk about looking at things from his perspective. These are people who have never been thrown against a wall by someone claiming to love them. There are *not* two sides to abusive situations. You did not cause it and you cannot make it stop. You can leave, though. And you should. I hope you do. And I hope you allow your divorce attorney to take the son of a bitch to the cleaners and otherwise hang 'em out to dry.

Familiarity, not survival, is the strongest drive in human beings. If it was survival, there would be no battered women. We want everything to be *the same* because it's what we *know*— even if it's terrible. Just because it's familiar doesn't make it good. Too often we just get used to something and fight like hell to believe that it's the way we want it to be, despite all evidence to the contrary.

There's more than one way to abuse a person. Ask anybody who's ever been married to an alcoholic, compulsive spender, sex addict, religious fanatic, workaholic, or drug addict.

Don't keep hurting yourself after someone else has hurt you. Sometimes the stuff we say to ourselves is way more destructive than what we've heard from someone else.

Your children know you're miserable. They live in the house with the misery, it's inescapable. How people can claim, on the one hand, that their children are the brightest, quickest, smartest people on the planet but at the same time think those same children are deaf, dumb (both mute *and* stupid), and blind to what's going on in the next room or on the other side of the dinner table, even—well, it's a mystery to me is all. The children think the misery's their fault. They're children and, by nature, totally egocentric—*everything* in their world revolves around them in their minds. They know you're miserable and they think they did something wrong and that they can fix it. They think they must keep your family together and will do anything to accomplish that—including jeopardizing their own future. If everybody's focusing on keeping them out of jail, there won't be time for fighting—that's the unconscious kid-logic at work.

Children, like everyone else, can deal very well with The Truth, no matter what it is—if it's *true*, they can deal. What makes people, little and otherwise, insane is lies and half-truths. When they see you crying and ask what's wrong and you say, "Nothing," that right there is crazy-making behavior. They can *see* you crying, which means to anybody with a brain that

something's not quite right, so what you are asking them to believe is what you *say*, which is in direct contradiction to what they can *see* with their own two eyes. If you think they won't carry that little lesson forward with them in their own lives, *you* are crazy. And you will be wondering—ten, fifteen, twenty years from now—why your daughter can't see for herself what a rotten piece of shit her cheating husband is—it's all right there in front of her. And then you'll remember who taught her to listen to empty words instead of believing her own experience. Oh, and you will suffer the tortures of the damned because your child is hurting and it's very hard to un-teach her what she spent her whole childhood learning—*from you.* And just wait until your precious darling son hits his wife for the first time—chip off the old block.

Many studies have shown the "damage" done to children by divorce. It would be very interesting to see studies done on the "damage" done to children by *living* with parents who despise each other. Children need good parents and role models, as many as they can get, and they don't need to associate with trash, whether they're related to it or not. Astonishingly, parents will allow their children to spend large amounts of unsupervised time with exes and other family members who engage in activities and lifestyles that would put any "friend" on the "out of bounds" list.

Yeah, yeah, yeah, you looove this guy. The more important question is whether or not you love *yourself* when you're

with him. Our beloved SPQ songstress Kacey Jones says, "I won't waste my tears on a man who makes me cry." And it should be noted that a man who's *worth* your tears won't make you cry them.

There is nothing in the vows about you eating shit. You never agreed to take whatever he dishes out.

Don't say you "can't stand" something when you are in a bad situation. You *are* standing it. You may be standing it on your head or under the bed, but time and events are proceeding along unabated. How you choose to "stand" something is optional. This is the part where you get to pick between "long-suffering" and taking action to help yourself.

If you ask him to change or stop a behavior and he says he's "trying," what he really means is "I am not doing anything any different and I have no intention of *ever* doing anything any different." When you invite somebody to come to a party you're having and they tell you they'll "try," what they really mean is, "No. I don't want to." Or "If I run out of every other thing I can conceivably do and I'm bored as shit, I might possibly show up, but don't count it." Now, they're grown up—right?—and independent, so if they get dressed, get in their car, head for your house and *want* to get there, chances are *excellent* that they'll end up there. That's what happens when they actually "try" to get there.

Change actually occurs in an instant. It might take you years and years and years and all manner of contortions to quit smoking cigarettes, but sooner or later, if you do quit, the last cigarette you smoked is the last cigarette you smoke. You don't light any more and stick 'em in your mouth.

Nobody changes anything until he's convinced he is about to lose something he's not prepared to live without. If he's engaging in behavior that is unacceptable to you and you tell him this, one of two things will happen: Either he'll be surprised to hear he's displeased you and he'll be sorry and say so and he'll never do it again (in other words, he'll change) or he'll keep doing it. He might bitch and moan or cuss and fuss or deny and justify, but—bottom line—he'll keep doing it. And you'll keep hating it, and the circle will go round and round until one of you steps off.

It doesn't matter how many fits you throw about his behavior—as long as you *stay*, you're saying it's okay by you. We've been taught to pay attention to what they do, not what they say. They were taught this, too. If he treats you like shit and you scream and yell about it, and still stay, what your actions say is, "I'd like some more please." When you finally say, and mean it, that this is unacceptable and you are through accepting it and therefore you are leaving—if he cares, he'll quit. Period. The end. And either way you win. Either he cares and he changes and y'all work it out and stay together and you're happy, or he doesn't care, doesn't change, and you leave and you're happy. The only way you can lose is by violating

your own standards and attempting or pretending to accept the unacceptable.

There is a Law of the Universe that says that everything, left alone, goes from order to disorder and disintegration. A brick left sitting in a vacant lot will turn to dust. A vacant house will fall in on itself, but if it's lived in, it will seemingly stand forever. I believe that this law applies to marriage.

I heard a story once about a young, newly married couple visiting the home of a very old, very long-married couple and seeing on the mantel a small wooden box, very nondescript in appearance but in such a place of prominence. The rest of the house was filled with all manner of exotic treasures from the couple's lifetime of travels together, and next to everything else, the little box seemed incongruous in its simplicity. When asked why such a simple wooden box was given such an important place in the house, the old woman replied, "It's our most treasured possession—it's our marriage box. When we were first married, fifty-five years ago, my mother gave us this box and told us it represented our marriage and we should put something into it every single day."

The young woman opened the box, found it empty and looked quizzically at the old couple. The old man answered, "Oh, there's nothing actually inside it, but we put it where we could always see it, and every time we look at it, we are reminded to do something *for* each other, every day—

whether it's me doing a chore I know she hates or her seeing that I've gotten in the shower without a towel again and putting one on the hook where I can reach it. It's just noticing what's needed and remembering to do little things for each other—paying attention to each other, in little ways, every day. And all those little things add up—just like money in the bank—so when you hit a rough patch, you've got something in there to fall back on and it'll carry you through to better days."

The Cutest Boy in the World and I have a marriage box. We like to think of it as our Divorce Prevention Box. It is *the most* hideous blue-and-peach-colored ceramic box with *dolphins* all over it, leaping and cavorting. (Our dear friends Allen Payne and Jeffrey Gross gave it to us because we have an ongoing fight with them over who can buy whom the most hideous gift, and they got *lots* of points for this purchase, lemme tell you.) We put it on top of the armoire in our bedroom, where it is the focal point of the whole room. We look at it every day, and even on the days when he might really like to smother me with a pillow before I wake up or I might want to hand him the hair dryer—in the shower—even on the days when we would like nothing better than to *smash* that butt-ugly box over the other one's head, we remember why it's there and we honor it. For one thing, it's danged hard to go to bed mad with that hideous thing leering at us from the top of the armoire. I mean, you gotta laugh when you look at it.

Now, granted, if you wake up one morning and find you are

in fact married to a psychopath, there ain't much you can do but run—and, boy hidee, I want you to run and run fast. Do not stay for one minute in an abusive situation. But most people don't wake up to nutcases. They simply fall asleep on the job and stop living in their marriages until it just decays, and one day the whole thing collapses in on them.

You may lose that relationship, but don't lose the lesson of it—it's yours to keep. If you learn from it, it was successful, regardless of the outcome. I hope this book will help you avoid divorces, but if it doesn't, I hope the laughing helps you heal. And you *know* sooner or later you're gonna look back on this whole deal and laugh about it—you know you are. You will get so much mileage with your girlfriends, telling all the crazy crap that guy did, y'all will be laughing your asses off at his expense. So, given that you know you're gonna laugh about it sooner or later, I say, get on over it and go on and pick *sooner.* If you cannot change it, you gotta either figure out how to make fun out of it or make fun *of* it, 'cause laughing is not just the best medicine for it, it's the *only* medicine.

Queen Debbie Mitchell has been lucky enough to have shared all of her nearly fifty rotations around the sun with her best friend, Rita. The two of them are devoted SPQ Wannabes and together they have formulated the theory of SPQ Lite. Lite is defined as the ability to take action to rise above anything that has cast a shadow over the heart of a Queen, and the Speed of Lite is how quickly that recovery can begin, simply by first remembering one's own Queenliness and acting accordingly. I

couldn't have said it better myveryownself. Here's wishing you a lifetime of laughter, love, and SPQ Lite.

Once upon a time, just the sound of his name made your panties hit the floor. And now the sight of him or even the sound of his voice makes you snarl at the man like a lesbian's dog. It happens. It's gonna be all right. Tiaras on, butts out, tits up, and move on, darlin'.

ACKNOWLEDGMENTS

I cannot begin to know what all goes into making this stuff into actual books after it leaves my feeble hands—but I know it's huge and it makes me tired just to think about it. I am profoundly and eternally grateful to everybody at Crown/Three Rivers/ Random House for taking a chance on an unknown humor writer from Mississippi. It has been a fine ride, indeed—thanks to the tireless work of JoAnne Prichard Morris, Sue Carswell, Steve Ross, Chip Gibson, Jenny Frost, Philip Patrick, Nina Frieman, Rachel Kahan, Dan Coppens, Carrie Thornton, Trisha Howell, Leta Evanthes, Camille Smith, Brandi Bowles, Lauren Dong, David Tran, Jill Flaxman, Linda Kaplan, and Amy Boorstein.

Even though I dog-cuss them regularly for the tortures they put me through on book tour, I am also grateful (on some level) to Brian Belfiglio and his evil henchman, Jay Sones.

Stephen Wallace and Johnny Evans are my heroes.

Muchas smoochas to my cute and crafty agent, Jenny Bent, and everybody at Trident Media Group.

Acknowledgments

Nothing at www.sweetpotatoqueens.com would ever get done if not for Alycia Jones and Sara Babin. Sometimes we even have to drag their husbands, Russell and Mike, into the fray and, thankfully, they don't resist too much.

I think we look especially cute on these covers and it's no accident—we had excellent help, for which we're grateful. Tom and Margaret Joynt are once again responsible for our darlin' photos. Tom for the photos—Margaret for the grins. Ashlee and Doug Douglass from Tuxes, Too are responsible for the snappy tux on The Cutest Boy in the World.

Many thanks to everybody at Hal & Mal's—Malcolm White, Hal White, Charly Abraham, and Anne Friday especially—for the Herculean effort that goes into the whole parade weekend—year after year after year after year.

Big smack to the staff at the Jackson Hilton—who are just crazy enough to WANT this crowd every year.

Thanks to all the many Queens I've come to know and love through your wonderful letters to me on the website and your incredible postings on messageboardoflove.com. Your strength becomes my own at times when I least expect it.

Melissa Manchester, Nancy Hasty, and Sharon Vaughn have been working night and day and everything in between writing *The Sweet Potato Queens Musical*. I am still incapable of articulating just how much this means to me, and let's just say, it takes a LOT to render ME speechless.

Kyle Jennings and the fabulous hard-working staff at Bad Dog Management—couldn't make it without you—wouldn't want to try.

Acknowledgments

I can never sufficiently thank the talented crew at the Cirlot Agency in Jackson, Mississippi, for their unending support and brilliant designs.

Randall Wallace wins the Fuchsia Braveheart Award for Best Performance in a Kilt at the 2005 St. Paddy's Parade. He won my own personal heart for being his own stupendous self and my friend.

I have come through a time of unspeakable heartbreak and I could not have made it without the folks who carried me. Blood kin and family by choice—they know who they are and the depth of my gratitude.

ALSO BY BOSS QUEEN JILL CONNER BROWNE

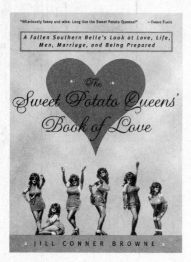

The bestselling book that introduced the world to the fun and glory that is the Sweet Potato Queens! From "The True Magic Words Guaranteed to Get Any Man to Do Your Bidding" to "What to Eat When Tragedy Strikes, or Just for Entertainment," this irreverent, shamelessly funny book is the *gen-u-wine* article.

0-609-80413-8. $13.95 paperback
Also available as a Random House audiobook:
0-553-75686-9. $25.95, unabridged,
    4 cassettes
0-7393-2056-4. $16.95, unabridged, 5 CDs

Less is more? Forget that, darling, because to Jill and all the Tammys, "more is more, and also better." From "Marriage—If You Must" to "More Death-Defying Recipes," this is the hilarious sequel to Jill Conner Browne's phenomenal debut, *The Sweet Potato Queens' Book of Love.*

0-609-80619-X. $13.95 paperback
Also available as a Random House
    audiobook:
0-553-75685-0. $25.95, unabridged,
    4 cassettes
0-7393-2057-2. $16.95, unabridged, 6 CDs

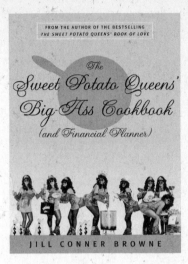

Now all fabulous women every-where can have their own mountains of royal fun and food, because Jill Conner Browne is revealing her top-secret recipes—and the events that inspired them. Dig in . . . to everything from the Gooiest Cake in the World to the justly infamous Pig Candy (that's bacon rolled in brown sugar). Financial advice, too!

0-609-80877-X. $13.95 paperback
Also available as a Random House
   audiobook:
0-7393-0226-4. $25.95, unabridged,
   4 cassettes
0-7393-2058-0. $16.95, unabridged, 5 CDs

The Sweet Potato Queens have devoted an inordinate amount of time to the pursuit of love, marriage, and great sex, and, honey, have they got some stories to tell! These stories are all in this hilarious (and highly instructive) handbook that shows you how to categorize any male as a "Bud Spud," "Scud Spud," "Pud Spud," or perhaps even the elusive "Spud Stud" (aka Mr. Right).

1-4000-4968-7. $13.95 paperback
Also available as a Random House audiobook:
0-7393-1503-X. $16.95, abridged, 2 cassettes
0-7393-1504-8. $16.95, abridged, 3 CDs

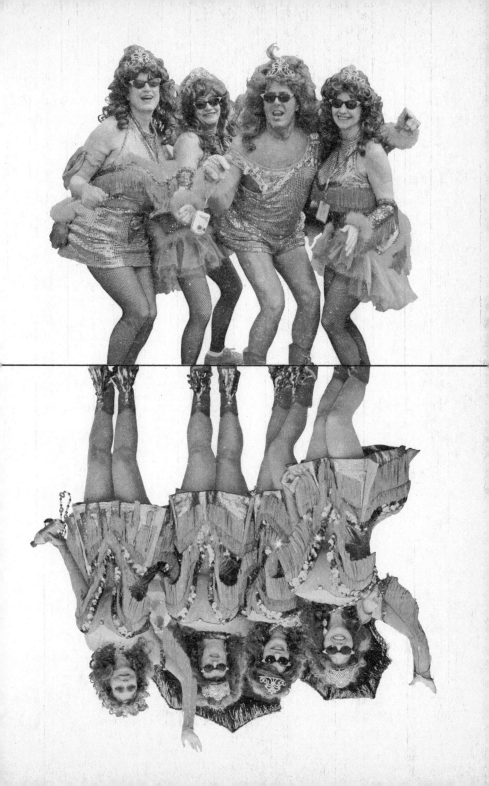